7 Day

University of Plymouth Library

C⸗ ⸗ring Questions & Answers: Employment Law

Michael J Boella, Marilyn Calabrese, Clifford Goodwin, Steven Goss-Turner

Croner Publications Ltd
Croner House
London Road
Kingston upon Thames
Surrey KT2 6SR
Telephone: 0181-547 3333

Published by
Croner Publications Ltd
Croner House
London Road
Kingston upon Thames
Surrey KT2 6SR
Tel: 0181-547 3333

While every care has been taken
in the writing and editing of this book,
readers should be aware that only Acts of Parliament
and Statutory Instruments have the force of law,
and that only the courts can authoritatively
interpret the law.

British Library Cataloguing-in-Publication Data.
A catalogue record for this book is available
from the British Library.

ISBN 1 85524 514 0

Printed by Creative Print and Design, Wales

INTRODUCTION

Of all the areas of law which a manager or owner in the hospitality industry will have to deal with, employment law is probably the most complex. Just over 30 years ago there was very little statute law (written law passed by Parliament) concerning employment; most of the employment relationship depended upon the common law of contract. This made it very difficult for employees to seek the protection of the law, not only because of the very high costs involved but also because the common law offered little protection to the servant, as employees were known.

The position today is fundamentally different as statute governs almost every aspect of the employment relationship. Statutory rights are enforced through industrial tribunals which provide a speedy, accessible and low-cost forum, offering a remedy of reinstatement as well as damages.

This pocket book sets out to answer a range of the key employment law questions that the owner or manager of a hotel, catering or similar business may have to answer. It could be said that employment law is the same for all businesses — of course, this is generally true. However, catering and all the related sectors of the hospitality industry have certain features which bring particular aspects of employment law to the fore. The seasonal nature and irregular hours of many catering and hotel operations as well as the mobile nature of many of the industry's workers create plenty of opportunities for legal misunderstanding about the nature of employers' and employees' rights and duties.

The book has been organised to correspond with the way that many personnel and human resource managers regard the employment relationship, ie from the metaphorical "cradle to the grave", or from the start of employment through to the end. Inevitably, there is some overlap between the various chapters but attempts have been made to keep any repetition to a minimum.

The authors are aware that in setting out to produce a concise summary, some aspects of the employment relationship may have been omitted or explained very simply. This is unavoidable in a brief book of this nature. However, more detailed information can be found in the associated works: *Croner's Catering* and *Croner's Catering Records and Procedures*. For those seeking an even deeper explanation and understanding of employment law, *Croner's Reference Book for Employers and Croner's Employment Law* will prove invaluable.

This book is intended as a guide and it is important to remember that no two cases are identical. Before taking any action, eg dismissing a long-serving employee, which may have legal consequences for you or your organisation, you should take professional legal advice.

THE AUTHORS

MICHAEL J BOELLA, MA, MIPD, MHCIMA, co-ordinating editor and contributor. Michael is a principal lecturer at the University of Brighton Business School where he specialises in teaching Hotel and Catering Studies. He was previously employed by Forte plc and Bass plc in personnel management roles and by Price Waterhouse as a management consultant. He is advisory editor of *Croner's Catering*.

MARILYN CALABRESE, FIPD, is a section editor of *Croner's Catering Records and Procedures* and Croner's Caterer's Briefing, specialising in employment matters. Marilyn is a freelance human resource consultant and director of a company of 100 employees. She previously worked for the Hotel and Catering Training Company as a training advisor and for J Lyons Catering as a personnel manager at their Gatwick Airport and City Airport catering outlets. Marilyn has been a tutor of Human Resource Management at the Universities of Brighton and Leicester, and has designed an Open Learning Course for the International Correspondence School (ICS).

CLIFFORD GOODWIN is a section editor of *Croner's Catering Records and Procedures* and an original contributor to *Croner's Management of Public Houses*. Clifford is a senior lecturer at the University of Brighton and a consultant specialising in Human Resource and Operations Management. His consultancy activities have focused on issues relating to the transfer of undertakings as a result of compulsory competitive tendering. Clifford is also a moderator for the HCIMA Diploma programme.

STEVEN GOSS-TURNER is a section editor of *Croner's Caterer's Briefing*. He is also a senior lecturer in the Department of Service Sector Management, part of the University of Brighton. Before embarking on a teaching career in 1991, he had been Training Director for the London and International division of Forte Hotels, a company with which he was associated for

15 years. Steven is author of *Managing People in the Hotel and Catering Industry*, published by Croner in 1992.

THE REVIEWERS

HELEN J DESMOND, LLB, LLM, is Lecturer in Law and Course Director, LLB by Part-time Studies, at the University of Buckingham.

JOHN STALLWORTHY, MBII FIPD, is a human resource consultant who has been head of personnel departments in a number of major international companies.

QUESTIONS

1. RECRUITMENT

Q1.1   When preparing a Personnel Specification to what extent am I allowed to discriminate by indicating a preference for one gender or the other?

Q1.2   Are there any legal obligations to advertise internally and externally for vacancies that occur?

Q1.3   What are the advantages of using an application form?

Q1.4   Is the application form a legally binding document?

Q1.5   When designing the application form, can I ask questions about the number and ages of any dependants the applicant may have?

Q1.6   Am I allowed to ask for a photograph?

Q1.7   How specific can I be in applying standards required for dress code, wearing jewellery, appearance, etc at an interview?

Q1.8   Is there any limitation on the questions I can ask in a reference application?

Q1.9   At what point in the recruitment process may I apply for references?

Q1.10   We have a predominantly "young" workforce; am I legally permitted to stipulate an age limit when recruiting employees?

Q1.11   What are my obligations regarding employing disabled persons?

Q1.12   Can I ask a job applicant whether they have a disability, and do workplaces have to be adapted for disabled employees?

Q1.13   Is there any legislation allowing me to discriminate positively in favour of female applicants?

Q1.14   During interviews I need to ascertain somebody's ability to attend work without having too many domestic problems such as responsibilities for children. How can I find out what I need to know without being discriminatory?

Q1.15   Can I legally discriminate against a person whose religious activities require them to attend certain services, festivals, etc which conflict with work requirements?

Q1.16   What does "indirect" discrimination mean as far as race/nationality is concerned?

Q1.17   Are there any circumstances under which I can specify that I want to employ a particular nationality or race?

2. GENERAL CONTRACT ISSUES

3. PAY AND BENEFITS

4. SICKNESS

5. MATERNITY ISSUES

9. RELATIONSHIPS WITH TRADE UNIONS

Q9.1 Is an employer obliged to recognise and negotiate with a trade union which claims to have a significant number of his or her employees as members?

Q9.2 Can I refuse to employ someone because of their membership of a trade union?

Q9.3 Can I refuse to employ someone because of their refusal to join a trade union?

Q9.4 Am I obliged to have a means of consulting with staff on any matters concerning their employment?

Q9.5 What information do employers have to give their employees about matters concerning their employment?

Q9.6 What information has to be given to a recognised trade union?

Q9.7 What rights to time off do union members have?

Q9.8 Can I dismiss someone because they took part in trade union activities at a time inconvenient to the business?

Q9.9 Can I dismiss someone because they took part in industrial activities, eg a strike?

Q9.10 Can a trade union be sued for damages arising from inducing breaches of contracts of employment?

Q9.11 Does the "closed" shop still exist?

Q9.12 As an employer am I obliged to help a union to conduct a ballot on our premises?

Q9.13 Is an employer obliged to operate a "check-off" system, ie collect union subscriptions on the union's behalf?

10. TRANSFER OF UNDERTAKINGS

Q10.1 If I am not a catering contractor, presumably these regulations do not apply to me. Is that correct?

Q10.2 If a ruling is made that there is a transfer of business and TUPE does apply, do I have to take on board all the staff's accrued benefits, etc?

Q10.3 Will TUPE apply in every situation regarding the "takeover" of a service?

Q10.4 If a catering or other contract changed hands, do the staff all have to be made redundant or could some be transferred?

Q10.5 At the time of a transfer of business, can an incoming contractor offer terms and conditions of service that are less favourable to the employees?

13. DISMISSAL

14. TERMINATING CONTRACTS

1. RECRUITMENT

Q1.1 **When preparing a Personnel Specification to what extent am I allowed to discriminate by indicating a preference for one gender or the other?**

A. The preparation of a Personnel Specification is part of the recruitment process and as such would be affected by the contents of the **Sex Discrimination Act 1975** (SDA) and **Race Relations Act 1976** (RRA) as well as the **Disability Discrimination Act 1995** (DDA). (See the answer to Q1.11, Q1.14 and Q1.20.)

Q1.2 **Are there any legal obligations to advertise internally and externally for vacancies that occur?**

A. There is no law concerning whether or where an organisation may advertise for new recruits. Often within the public sector (Local Government, Civil Service) there has been a policy adopted that all positions must be advertised externally even if it is evident that a suitable candidate exists within the organisation.

This practice which has the advantage of drawing from a greater "pool", bringing in new knowledge, skills and ideas needs to be weighed against the effect on the workforce of promotion or transfer opportunities.

Q1.3 **What are the advantages of using an application form?**

A. The main advantage is that all the information you require is set out in a standard format in the order that you have chosen and as such saves a lot of time. It also contains information you may wish to elicit fairly from all candidates that may not appear on a cv, eg driving licence information, why they think they are suitable for the job, etc. If handwriting and accuracy is one of the relevant criteria for a job, an application form may provide an employer with a first impression of neatness, etc.

Completing an application form requires more time and may sift out a few candidates who are less committed to the job advertised. It enables an employer to compare like with like and in this way can be less discriminatory.

Q1.4   Is the application form a legally binding document?

A.   Usually an application form asks the applicant to sign and verify that all the information disclosed is true. This being the case, the usual application of contractual law, including the **Misrepresentation Act 1967** can be applied. (See Q1.12 and Q1.20.)

Q1.5   When designing the application form, can I ask questions about the number and ages of any dependants the applicant may have?

A.   There is no law in the UK to stop an organisation presenting questions concerning family dependants in an application form, or indeed at an interview. However, an employer should be able to justify *why* the question is being asked, and ensure that *all* applicants are asked the same question. If a claim of sex discrimination were lodged against an employer who sought this information, the onus would lay with the employer to prove that no discrimination had taken place and that there had been another perfectly sound reason for not offering this applicant the position available. The more important question would be — "Is this person able to take on the full responsibilities of the job?" Part of those responsibilities include attendance. It is certainly not acceptable and would be contravening the SDA (direct discrimination) if an employer did not offer a female applicant a position because it was assumed that she would not be able to attend work at certain times. (See also Q1.14 and Q1.18.)

Q1.6   Am I allowed to ask for a photograph?

A.   There is no law to prevent you asking for a photograph. However, good practice would be to ask the question — "Why is a photograph essential?" If a discriminatory claim were made on the grounds of sex or race following an application for a post, it may not help the case. If an employer's argument is that "appearance" is important, then it would be wise to clarify this in the personnel specification. (See Q1.17 and Q1.18.)

Q1.7   How specific can I be in applying standards required for dress code, wearing jewellery, appearance, etc at an interview?

A.   Appropriateness

Rules may be set out that are considered reasonable for the type of operation of the business with, for example, due consideration of a "conventional" image, if required. In general, tribunals accept that certain styles may be unacceptable to most customers in certain types of business. However, care should be taken to avoid any discriminatory aspects when setting standards on the wearing of rings, earrings and hair length particularly, and adopt the same appearance codes for both sexes as much as possible. Public perception of acceptability is constantly changing and employers need to regularly review these rules.

Race

In addition to ensuring that dress codes are not discriminatory on the grounds of sex, employers also need to be aware of religious requirements. For example, Sikhs have special dispensation to allow them to wear a turban instead of a safety helmet (s.11 **Employment Act 1989**). A ban on beards would exclude all orthodox Sikhs (although, in certain cases, may be acceptable on the grounds of hygiene).

There have been a number of cases concerning hair length, the wearing of earrings and the application of a dress code in the last few years. In the *Smith v Safeway plc* 1995 IRLR 132 case, a delicatessen assistant was dismissed because his ponytail had grown too long to fit under his hat. Company rules were that men's hair was required to be above their shirt collars; women could have shoulder length hair provided it was tied back. Mr Smith claimed this amounted to direct discrimination in breach of s.1(1)(a) of the SDA. His claim was upheld by the Employment Appeals Tribunal (EAT), who took the view that the employee's treatment had been less favourable and that the employer's requirements could be applied equally to both sexes without restricting men's hair length.

A previous case concerning a woman who wished to wear trousers in the bookshop where she was employed (*Schmidt v Austicks Bookshops Ltd* 1977 IRLR 360) was not upheld on the basis that the EAT considered that rules about dress may be applied even if those rules may be different for males and females. In this case, female employees were only permitted to wear trousers in the stockroom and not where they could be seen by customers. The EAT ruled that no comparable provision could be applied to male employees. Since then a more recent case concerning a transvestite taxi driver, who claimed (but lost) that his employer had discriminated against him for not allowing him to wear a skirt to work. It was deemed to be "inappropriate" in a businesslike environment.

In the *Smith v Safeway* case the final view (although divided) was taken that a restriction on hair length affected a person at all times, unlike other rules on appearance (eg a dress code which concerns working hours only).

Q1.8   Is there any limitation on the questions I can ask in a reference application?

A.   Strictly speaking, no there is not. However, any employer seeking a reference (as well as providing one) must bear in mind that the referee is legally bound against making untrue allegations which may harm another person's reputation with others.

As far back as 1936 (*Sim v Stretch* 52 TLR 669) defamation of character has been defined as "the publication of a statement about a person which reflects on a person's reputation". This includes in writing (or film, video, etc) or by word of mouth (also gestures, and sounds).

More recently the House of Lords held that an employer is under a "duty of care" to a former employee when providing a reference. (*Spring v Guardian Assurance plc* 1994 IRLR 460 — see *Croner's Catering Newsletter No. 41*).

A prospective employer may find it useful to receive tangible factual information apertaining to the employee's attendance, punctuality, etc but more "subjective" information concerning attitudes may depend on the motivation of the employee, the job they were doing and who they worked with, etc.

Q1.9   At what point in the recruitment process may I apply for references?

A.   This will depend upon procedures and preferences for an organisation. Many public sector organisations apply for references prior to the interview (or other means of selection), most organisations appear to apply following the interview, and may even apply after the person has commenced employment. Whichever method is used, it is essential to ensure that the permission of the applicant is sought first. This may be via the application form, asked at the interview, or the offer of employment may be made subject to satisfactory references being received.

Q1.10   We have a predominantly "young" workforce; am I legally permitted to stipulate an age limit when recruiting employees?

A.   At the time of going to print, no legislation exists in the UK to prevent employers from discriminating on the basis of age when they recruit staff. So far, the Government has rejected calls for legislation on age discrimination. However, the current demographic trends (a quarter of the population is over 55 years of age and two million of the three million plus unemployed are over the age of 45) are to continue into the next decade. Some other countries have introduced age discrimination laws, including the USA and Canada, France, and some Australian states. The IPD published a set of guidelines in 1990 to encourage practising professional personnel managers to consider older applicants more actively. It is therefore very likely that this situation will be addressed in the near future. Many public sector employers now set out to prevent age discrimination by not asking for age or date of birth.

Q1.11 **What are my obligations regarding employing disabled persons?**

A. Employers with more than 15 employees are subject to the **Disability Discrimination Act 1995**. The Disability Discrimination Act defines a "disabled person" as someone who has a "physical or mental impairment which has a substantial and long term adverse effect on his ability to carry out normal day to day activities". Long term is further defined as being a period of 12 months, and even if the impairment ceases to have a substantial adverse effect, if there is a likelihood of the effect re-occurring then it is to be treated as continuing.

Affecting normal day to day activities includes affecting any one of the following:

- manual dexterity
- physical co-ordination
- continence
- mobility
- ability to lift, carry or otherwise move everyday objects
- speech, hearing or eyesight
- memory or ability to learn or understand
- perception of the risk of physical danger.

This is even so where the disability may be controlled by medication or special aids. A diabetic would therefore be included within this definition as would a person suffering from cancer or MS.

The Act makes it unlawful to discriminate

- during recruitment
- in the terms and conditions of employment
- in the opportunities for training or promotion or any other benefits
- when terminating employment or subjecting him/her any other detriment.

It also imposes a duty to make "reasonable adjustments" (see Q1.12)

Discriminatory treatment of disabled persons may be justified if in the employer's opinion:

- the disabled person is unsuitable for the job
- the disability significantly impedes performance in the job
- the value of training would be significantly reduced by the nature of the disability.

It must, however, be reasonable for the employer to hold this opinion. Complaints of unlawful disability discrimination will be heard by employment tribunals, which will be able to award compensation on the same basis as for sex or race discimination.

Q1.12 Can I ask a job applicant whether they have a disability, and do workplaces have to be adapted for disabled employees?

A. Many application forms traditionally asked whether the applicant had a disability. With the introduction of the **Disability Discrimination Act 1995**, if an employer retains this question a statement should be included explaining why the question is being asked (eg to be aware of any adjustments that may be required in the workplace, or if any specific types of disability would be unsuitable for the vacant position). There should also be a statement in the corresponding advertisements that applications from disabled persons are welcome. Any questions in the interview should be specifically tailored to ascertain the applicant's ability to do the job

(eg "This would be your job description; would you have any problems performing the required tasks?")

The **Disability Discrimination Act** requires employers to make "reasonable adjustments". Interpretation will vary according to the type, and possibly size, of the business. Failure to make such an adjustment may result in a claim of discrimination against the company. Statistics show that most adjustments required are minor and cost hundreds rather than thousands of pounds (eg loose equipment such as voice-activated PC's, etc).

Further Information

Published Guidelines on how employers can comply with the Act are available from the DDA Information Line, tel: 0345 622633.

Q1.13 **Is there any legislation allowing me to discriminate positively in favour of female applicants?**

A.   There is no legal quota scheme for the employment of men or women, although there have been voluntary initiatives to target females in the workplace particularly at managerial level (eg Opportunity 2000, an initiative developed in the early 1990s).

Under the **Sex Discrimination Act 1975** it is unlawful to discriminate on the grounds of gender or on the grounds that a person is married. Sex discrimination by an employer is defined as follows.

1.   **Direct discrimination** is where a person is or would be treated less favourably than someone of the opposite gender.

2.   **Indirect discrimination** is applying a requirement or condition which is:

   (a)   such that the proportion of women that can comply is considerably smaller than the proportion of men

   (b)   not justifiable

   (c)   to the woman's detriment because she cannot comply (s.1(1)(b) of the SDA).

(All of these apply equally to men and women, although the number of cases of sex discrimination against men still remains extremely low.)

The Act covers discrimination at recruitment and selection stage as well as during and at the termination of employment.

Q1.14 **During interviews I need to ascertain somebody's ability to attend work without having too many domestic problems such as responsibilities for children. How can I find out what I need to know without being discriminatory?**

A. As long as the same information is solicited from all applicants regardless of sex an employer may be seen to be fair. There is often a general assumption amongst employers in this country that it is the female's responsibility to look after their children if required. In practice, it is becoming more common for males to be single parents, or to take joint responsibility for their family. It is unlawful to assume a male is the breadwinner of a family (*Coleman v Skyrail Oceanic Ltd* 1981 IRLR 398).

Q1.15 **Can I legally discriminate against a person whose religious activities require them to attend certain services, festivals, etc which conflict with work requirements?**

A. Section 3 of the RRA prohibits discrimination against a person on the grounds of colour, race, nationality or ethnic or national origins.

An "ethnic group" is defined as having two characteristics:

- a long shared history
- a cultural tradition of its own, often but not necessarily associated with religious observance.

Other relevant characteristics include:

- common ancestry
- common language
- common literature
- common religion

- being a minority, oppressed or dominant group.

(*Mandla v Lee and others* 1983 IRLR 209.)

This means that Sikhs, Jews and gypsies, for example, fit the criteria but Rastafarians and Muslims do not.

Q1.16 **What does "indirect" discrimination mean as far as race/nationality is concerned?**

A.   See also answer to Q1.13.

The **Race Relations Act 1976** defines indirect discrimination in the same way as the SDA. This is applied if the condition means that the proportion of persons from the same racial group is considerably smaller than the proportion not of that racial group — ie it is not a case of comparing racial groups, but of comparing a specific racial group with the population as a whole. For example, a requirement for a red-haired person could be shown to represent a smaller proportion of black Afro-Carribeans than the proportion of the population as a whole.

If a condition is justifiable irrespective of a racial group then there is no discrimination. The onus is upon the employer to prove justifiability.

If a requirement is to the detriment of one particular racial group because they cannot comply with it, this may be construed as indirect discrimination.

Q1.17 **Are there any circumstances under which I can specify that I want to employ a particular nationality or race?**

A.   The **Race Relations Act 1977** outlines a number of genuine occupational qualifications (GOQ's) under which circumstances it is legal to specify. These are:

- for entertainment/dramatic performances
- artists/photographic models
- personal services for the welfare of a particular ethnic group, eg Health Visitor

- authenticity, eg Asian waiting staff in a Chinese restaurant.

The last circumstance is the most likely to occur within the catering industry. It should be noted that a Chinese chef for a Chinese restaurant would be unlikely to fall into this category unless the kitchen were an open style (visible to the customers) and therefore forming part of the atmosphere.

Q1.18 **Are there any circumstances under which I can specify that I want to employ a female or a male?**

A. The **Sex Discrimination Act** states a list of genuine occupational qualifications (GOQ's) as follows:

- physiology (as opposed to physical stamina)
- decency/privacy
- promotion of welfare/education
- single sex institutions, eg all-female health club, gentleman's club
- accommodation provided with the job, eg if there are limited bathroom facilities, an employer may fairly choose to retain the accommodation within one house as single sex — this may in turn limit the employer in whom he or she may recruit. However, it is likely to only be considered reasonable if the policy was consistent over a period of time
- if the job is outside the UK and local laws and customs would significantly constrain a woman in achievement of the job, eg Saudi Arabia.

Employment of a married couple

It is legal for an employer to state that he or she requires/ prefers a legally married couple. This has been particularly common in the past for pub management. In practice, it is becoming increasingly less common.

Q1.19 **Is there a minimum size of organisation that is not covered by sex and race discrimination legislation?**

A. No, it applies to all organisations dealing with job applicants, employees, contracted workers, partners and other self-employed persons who may be working for an organisation.

Q1.20 **If an employee has been convicted of a criminal offence in the past, what rights do I have as an employer to have access to this information?**

A. Under the **Rehabilitation of Offenders Act 1974**, a person who has become rehabilitated shall be treated as a person who has not committed or been charged with or prosecuted for or convicted of or sentenced for the offence which was the subject of that conviction.

An employee or prospective employee has the right to conceal details relating to what is called a "spent" conviction. Therefore, once a conviction is "spent" that person is not required by law to answer any questions concerning their past which cannot be answered without acknowledging or referring to the spent conviction. Failure to disclose a spent conviction cannot be used as grounds for dismissal or discrimination in any way. Gaps in employment history that may appear in a candidate's application may be explored but without an aim to discriminate. Any other person who knows about the conviction (including an employer, or previous employer) is also protected for failing to disclose the information. Periods of time after which a conviction is spent vary according to the seriousness of the offence; some convictions are never spent. Some professions are excluded from this protection and candidates always have to disclose previous convictions; these include accountants, nurses, doctors and solicitors. (See Croner's *Catering*, section 4, for details.)

Q1.21   What rights do I have to impose a medical on applicants when recruiting and to what extent can I allow this to affect my decision on employment?

A.   It is common practice for larger organisations to impose a health check upon job applicants these days, although they are by no means necessary for all jobs. If a decision is made not to employ somebody on the basis of a medical check alone, it must be relevant to the employment. Any recourse to dismissal must be clearly stated within the main statement of terms and conditions of employment. This may be particularly relevant for food handlers who may be, for example, salmonella carriers or who suffer from a serious skin complaint, etc.

Q1.22   What permits are required these days for potential employees both from within the EU and other countries?

A.   The employment of European Union nationals does not require the authorisation of the Employment Department. These rights are embodied in Article 48 of the Treaty of Rome. The following countries are at present Member States: Austria, Belgium, Denmark, Finland, France, Germany, Greece, Italy, Luxembourg, The Netherlands, Portugal, Republic of Ireland, Spain, Sweden, and the UK (including Gibraltar). Non-EU nationals who are subject to immigration control must have a work permit issued by the Employment Department unless they fall into one of the limited permit-free categories (eg Commonwealth citizens who can prove that one grandparent was born in the UK). The prospective employer must obtain the permit for a specific job, before the person enters the country, by completing form WP1. A permit will not be granted if, in the opinion of the Employment Department, suitable resident labour is available to fill the post or if the conditions of employment offered are less favourable than those offered in the area for similar work. The scheme is therefore aimed at workers of degree level or who have specialist skills or qualifications.

Permits are normally issued for a limited period of up to four years.

Q1.23 **What are the implications of the Asylum and Immigration Act 1996?**

A. The Act came into effect on 27 January 1997 and is intended to ensure that only those who are legally entitled are offered employment. Employers can be held liable for any illegal workers and can be fined a maximum penalty for this criminal offence (currently £5000 for each person being employed illegally).

You can protect yourself by making certain basic checks before taking on new employees and ask to see (and copy) one of the following:

- a document issued by a previous employer, the Inland Revenue, the Benefits Agency, the Contributions Agency or the Employment Service which states the National Insurance number of the person named
- a passport or national identity card issued by a Member State of the EU and which describes the holder as a national of that State
- a passport describing the holder as having the right of abode in the UK
- a certificate of registration or naturalisation as a British citizen
- a birth certificate issued in the UK or Republic of Ireland
- a passport or other travel document endorsed to show that the person named is exempt from immigration control, has indefinite leave to enter or remain in the UK, or current leave and is not precluded from taking the employment in question, or has no time limit on their stay
- a letter issued by the Home Office confirming the same
- a passport or other travel document endorsed to show that the holder has a current right of residence in the UK as a family

member of a named national of a Member State of the EC and who is resident in the UK

- a letter issued by the Immigration and Nationality Directorate or Home Office indicating that the person is a British citizen or has permission to take employment

- a work permit or other approval issued by the Department for Employment and Education

- a passport describing the holder as a British Dependent Territories citizen (having a connection with Gibraltar).

You do not need to, and should not, make checks on employees who were working for you before 27 January 1997.

Q1.24 Are there any advantages of using psychometric tests as part of the selection process?

A. The whole question of whether to use some form of psychometric testing, particularly for management recruitment and development, is one of some debate.

The IPD first published a Code of Practice on Occupational Testing in 1989. The British Psychological Society have set test standards for the various tests on the market. Only some tests meet these standards. They can vary from answering anything between 50 and 500 questions and take anything from 10–15 minutes to several hours to administer. The armed forces have been using them for years for officer selection. Some large organisations employ a trained psychologist to interpret the results and interview the applicants, whilst others may be administered by personnel with limited training. Overall it would seem that they can be of use as a support to other means of selection (ie interview), but in general it is not viewed favourably by the professional bodies concerned that they be used as an isolated initial means of selection.

Q1.25   Are there any discriminatory implications of using psychometric tests as part of the selection process?

A.   There has been considerable concern over the fairness of selection and assessment testing in relation to equal opportunities. What has been revealed is that whilst properly constructed tests have been found to predict job success better than any other measure, they may not truly reflect the abilities of ethnic minority groups, or may contain a gender bias towards males. *Saville & Holdsworth Ltd* have published a set of guidelines in conjunction with the CRE and EOC, *Equal Opportunities Guidelines for Best Test Practice in the Use of Personnel Selection Tests*.

An example case was the use of a verbal reasoning test used by British Rail for driver applicants which was found to have a disadvantageous effect upon those who spoke English as their second language.

Q1.26   What are the legal implications if, having entered a contract with an employment agency, the new recruit doesn't stay?

A.   An employment agency should have a set of standard terms and conditions of business which they will present to any prospective customer. In addition to this, they may encourage an employer to enter a specific customised contract with them which may provide the employer with preferential commission rates, and the agency with a guaranteed "head start" as and when any vacancies arise.

As with any contract entered into, the answer to this question will depend upon what has been agreed. This may be in the form of a contract or simply a letter of a more general nature, with the agreement being the general terms and conditions of business that the agency uses. Agencies may have a minimum introduction fee and usually charge a percentage of the salary being paid, which varies according to the level of the position. They will usually include a scale of rebates if the employment is terminated within the first few weeks of employment. It is advisable to read the small print before entering into any agreement, and negotiate terms if desirable.

Q1.27 If I employ staff from an agency, are they employees of our organisation?

A. This may depend upon frequency of work and length of service (*BP Chemical v Gillick and Roevin Management Services Ltd*). It may be deemed that the organisation is the "principal" employer and has an employment relationship with the employee. If this is the case then some legislation will be seen to apply.

 If the staff are seen to be contracted workers, some legislation still applies. (See Q1.11, Q1.14, Q1.15.)

Q1.28 What restrictions are there for the employment of persons under the age of 18 within the catering industry?

A. The employment of young persons, ie those under 18 but over school leaving age, is controlled by the following legislation.

Employment of Women, Young Persons and Children Act 1920

Children and Young Persons Act 1933-69 (as amended by the **Children (Protection at Work) Regulations 1998**)

Working Time Regulations 1998

In addition the **Working Time Regulations 1998** have included specific restrictions to the employment of young persons, distinct from adult worker requirements. These are:

1. A young worker is entitled to a *48 hour* rest period in any 7 day period.

2. A young worker is entitled to *12 hours* or consecutive rest in any 24 hour period.

3. Young workers are entitled to a rest break of 30 minutes if they work more than *4.5 hours* in a day.

Q1.29 What restrictions are there for the employment of children (under 16)?

No child may be employed:

- under the age of 14 (one of the main debates between Britain and the rest of the EC when the Social Charter was formulated)
- during school hours
- before 0700 hrs and after 1900 hrs
- for more than two hours during any school day
- for more than two hours on a Sunday
- to lift, carry or move anything so heavy as to be likely to cause injury to him or her.

It is advisable to contact the local Careers Office or JobCentre for details of any byelaws and any exceptions that may exist which may affect the employment of children under 16 years of age.

2. GENERAL CONTRACT ISSUES

Q2.1 **What is a contract of employment?**

A. Many employers and managers do not distinguish between what is known as the "Statement of Main Terms and Conditions of Employment" as required by the **Employment Rights Act 1996** and what is, in effect, the common law contract.

The common law contract is much wider-ranging than the "written statement" required by the Act. The common law contract consists of the offer made by the employer which may possibly include a range of terms and conditions deriving possibly from the original advertisement, statements made at interview and at induction, company documents such as "house rules", job descriptions, trade practices, etc. In addition, the contract may have been modifed over time by new conditions being agreed by both parties. It may also incorporate terms and conditions agreed with a recognised trade union.

The "written statement" required by the Act has to include a number of specified conditions and has to be given to an employee within two months of starting employment. The written statement is *not*, in itself, a "contract of employment".

Because of this it is good practice to issue a full contract of employment (incorporating everything required by the Act) and all other important conditions before an employee starts employment. The employee should be asked to sign and return a copy as acceptance.

A contract of employment, in most respects, comes within the scope of the common law of contract. Contract law specifies that for a contract to be enforceable there must be a number of essentials. The most important of these are; offer, acceptance, consideration (something of value such as money or work), and the intention to enter into a legally binding agreement.

This means that a contract may arise in a number of different ways. For example, at its simplest, a contract of employment could be entered into during a telephone conversation. It could be the result of an interview or an exchange of letters. At the other extreme a contract of employment could be the result of protracted negotiations involving offers and counter offers and an extensive range of conditions being agreed upon (as might be the case with the contracts of highly paid sportsmen).

A contract of employment has to be distinguished from a contract for services and the penalties for not making such a distinction can be very heavy, particularly for the employer. The distinction will be discussed below.

Q2.2 **What are my general duties as an employer to my employees?**

A. Many of an employer's duties to its employees are defined by the employment contract, by statute or by case law, most of which will be expanded through the course of this pocketbook.

The consequences of being in breach of these legal obligations are that the employee, if suffering damage or injury, can sue for damages. Two recent and important examples include that of protecting employees from sexual or racial harassment. Another is that of "stigma" damages, (see below) *(Malik and another v Bank of Credit and Commerce SA (BCCI) 1997 IRLR 462)*.

The principal obligations are as follows.

1. *The duty to pay.* Where no wages have been agreed the courts may imply reasonable remuneration into the contract of employment, bearing in mind any minimum wage legislation.

2. *The duty to provide work.* Generally speaking, so long as an employer pays its employee it is not obliged to provide work, ie it can lay off staff on full pay (or as agreed by contract). The

general principle on the implied duty to provide work was stated in *Collier v Sunday Referee Publishing Co. Ltd* (1940) 2 KB 647.

In some cases there is an obligation to provide work, particularly where the amount to be earned by the employee is determined by the amount of work done. Other cases might be when the employee needs to work to enhance his or her reputation or where damage could be done to a person's professional reputation should it become known that he or she was not working.

3. *Health and safety.* Whilst most health and safety issues are now covered by statute and regulations, there are still common law contractual duties placed upon an employer concerning employees' health and safety. This duty is considered to contain three basic elements:

   (a) to select reasonably competent employees

   (b) to provide adequate materials

   (c) to provide a safe system of working.

If the employer is in breach of any of the above and the employee suffers injury, he or she could sue the employer for damages. The employee could also resign. The employer could also be prosecuted under Health and Safety legislation.

THE DUTY OF REASONABLENESS

There is a duty on both parties to be reasonable and to do nothing that would undermine the mutual confidence of the two parties to the contract.

The duty of mutual trust and confidence

In 1997 a landmark case developed the concept of mutual trust and confidence by awarding "stigma" damages. In this case two employees were unable to find new employment after the failure of the employer and as a direct result of the employer's discredited reputation *(Malik and another v Bank of Credit and Commerce SA* (BCCI) 1997 IRLR 462).

Q2.3 **What are the general duties owed by an employee to his or her employer?**

A. Again, most duties will be defined by the contract itself or by statute. However, courts over the years have developed some general principles as follows.

1. *The duty to serve.* This means that the employee has an obligation to serve the employer within the terms of the employment contract. The relationship of an employer and employee, under a contract of service, is a *personal* one, ie an employee cannot delegate to another person (although it is not uncommon in some situations for employees to send members of their family or friends to cover for them). There is no obligation on the employee to be at the employer's disposal all the time — but only within the terms of the contract.

2. *The duty to be obedient.* An employee is under a duty to be obedient — but this does not mean that an employer can ask him or her to do anything it wants. The employee must, however, obey lawful orders that are within the terms of the employment contract.

3. *Competence and duty of care.* With few exceptions (eg where training is to be provided) an employee promises that he or she is competent to do the work involved. As a consequence, lack of competence may be a breach of contract which could lead to dismissal and even (in extreme circumstances) to an action for damages.

4. *Duty of good faith.* The relationship between an employer and employee is one of good faith. This is divided into a number of different duties.

(a) *Secret profits.* The employee must not accept secret profits or commissions. This is quite common in the hospitality industry with employees responsible for purchasing supplies often being given "backhanders" or gifts. An employee is obliged to inform the employer of such gifts, etc. Failure to do so could enable the employer to dismiss the employee for breach of contract.

(b) *Confidential information.* An employee must not pass on confidential information to the employer's competitors.

(c) *Inventions and copyright.* Copyright and patents made in the course of employment are normally the property of the employer — although some employment contracts provide for these to remain the property of the employee. (**Copyright Act 1956** and **Patent Act 1977**.)

(d) *Disclosure of breach of duty.* Employees, particularly those in positions of responsibility, may be under a duty to disclose the breaches of duty of another employee.

Q2.4   How can I distinguish between an employee and a contractor such as a gardener working for me, a window cleaner or even a "homeworker"?

A.   It is not always easy to determine if someone working is an employee or a subcontractor. The distinction, however, is vital because in the case of subcontractors they are responsible for their own tax affairs whereas in the case of employees the employer is responsible. Should inland revenue decide that a "subcontractor" is in fact an employee, the back tax and penalties can be considerable.

Section 30 of the **Employment Rights Act 1996** defines an employee as an individual who has entered into or works under a contract of employment. A contract of employment is also defined as a contract of service. However, to determine if someone is really an employee in law, a number of tests have been developed by the courts over the years. The main ones are as follows.

1. *The control test.* In general this tests the extent to which the "employer" has control over the worker in question. A worker works sufficiently under the control of an employer to qualify as an *employee* if the employer not only instructs the worker what to do, but also how and when to do it (*Yewens v Noakes* (1880) 6 QBD 580). Clearly, employees such as waitresses or bar staff would fall under the definition of "employee" when the control test is applied. It is much less clear when applied, for example, to a gardener, a window cleaner or a musician who may all also work for other people during the same week. (See also *Lane v Shire Roofing Company (Oxford) Ltd* [1995] IRLR 493.)

2. *The business integration test.* To what extent is the work of the worker an integral part of the business? Clearly a cook working for a restaurant is integral, or central, to the business whereas a window cleaner's or a musician's work is an accessory or ancillary to it. (*Stevenson Jordan and Harrison Ltd v Macdonald and Evans* (1952)1 TLR (CA).) In contrast, a musician working for an orchestra may well be deemed an employee because the business of the orchestra is music (*Whittaker v Minister for Pensions and National Insurance* (1966) 3 All ER 531).

3. *The multiple test.* The multiple test adopts a broad approach — the definition not relying on a single factor. So the multiple test would expect that:

    (a) the worker agrees to provide his or her own work and skill to the "employer" in return for a wage or other remuneration

    (b) that he or she will be subject to the other's control

    (c) the other provisions of the contract are consistent with it being a contract of service *(Ready-Mixed Concrete*

(SouthEast) Ltd v Minister of Pensions and National Insurance (1968) 1 All ER (QBD).

HOMEWORKERS — POSSESSION OF OWN MACHINERY

In the case of "homeworkers", eg someone who regularly cooks food in their own home for transfer to a restaurant or pub, it is important to establish if the relationship is one of employment. For there to be an employment relationship there should be some form of obligation on both sides, ie to give and to accept work. This does not exist in a straightforward sale of goods — neither side is obliged to sell or to buy. However, if there was a "well-founded expectation because there was a regular giving and taking of work over a period of years" an employment relationship may exist. (*Nethermere (St Neotts Limited v Taverna & Gardner* 1984 IRLR 240.)

Q2.5 **How can I distinguish between a full-time employee and a part-time employee?**

A. Until recently many employers distinguished, in practice, between full-time and part-time employees mainly through the number of hours worked and through offering different conditions. Today, no clear distinction exists. As a rough guideline, full-time employees tend to work a five day week of around 30–45 hours, for about 48 weeks a year. Part-time employees may work for as little as one session a week involving as little as three or four hours.

Following a European Court decision, both full-time and part-time employees are now supposed to benefit, pro rata (where relevant), from similar conditions such as the right to written particulars and itemised pay statements, minimum statutory notice, time off for public and trade union duties, maternity leave, holiday entitlements and pay, sick pay, pension schemes **(Employment Protection (Part-time Employees) Regulations 1995** (SI 1995 No. 31). See Table 1 for a list of rights in employment.

Q2.6   How can I distinguish between a part-time employee and a casual worker?

A.   In essence a casual worker is one that works on a contract for a limited period such as one evening session in a bar, or for ten days for a special occasion such as an hotel Christmas programme. This is to be distinguished from workers who have agreed to work regularly, for example, every Saturday evening. In the definitive case the Court of Appeal ruled that casuals were not regular employees because:

– the engagement was terminable without notice

– the worker had the right to accept or to refuse the work

– the company was not obliged to provide work

(*O'Kelly and Others v Trusthouse Forte plc* (1983)).

This is to be contrasted with workers who might be on "zero hour" contracts under which the employer is obliged to offer work to the worker when suitable work arises and the worker is obliged to accept the offer (*Carmichael v National Power plc* The Times, 2 April, 1998, CA). In this case it was found that the employment was continuous and covered the whole period and not just the periods of work. This judgment has serious implications for the hospitality industry which relies heavily on "casual" staff who can be called at short notice to come into work.

Q2.7   Is it important to be able to make such distinctions?

A.   It is extremely important to distinguish between casual workers and other regular workers. Workers employed on regular contracts, have a range of rights which an employer is obliged to meet. Casual workers, even those who work often for an employer (but on session by session contracts) have no such rights. In the case of casual workers an employer's commitments end (apart from income tax and national insurance obligations) at the end of the work session concerned. In the case of regular workers this is not so.

Furthermore, an employer could be responsible for injury for certain categories of people it may have thought to be or intended to be "contractors" (*Lane v Shire Roofing Company (Oxford) Ltd* [1995] IRLR 493).

Qualifying Continuous Service for Employees' Rights

Right	Minimum Service
Protection from discrimination on grounds of race, sex or disability	None
Statement of terms and conditions of employment	1 month*
Pay during medical suspension	1 month
Guarantee payments	1 month
Right to union membership and to take part in union activities	None
Time off work for: union duties	None
union activities	None
safety representatives	None
public duties	None
redundant employees	2 years
ante-natal care	None
Statutory maternity pay: lower rate	26 weeks
higher rate	26 weeks
Right to return to work after maternity absence:	
extended maternity leave	2 years †
basic maternity leave	None
Itemised pay statement	None
Written reasons for dismissal	2 years
Minimum notice of termination of employment	1 month
Right not to be unfairly dismissed	2 years
Redundancy pay	2 years
Paid annual leave	13 weeks

Notes

* The statement must be issued within two months of the start of employment.
† Unless the organisation has less than five employees.

EMPLOYMENT TRIBUNALS

Employment Tribunals (formerly Industrial Tribunals) were first created by the **Industrial Training Act 1964** to deal with employers' appeals against assessment to levy by industrial training boards. Their scope was, though, radically extended in 1971 and again in 1974.

Their function now is also to provide an informal and speedy method for employees to enforce their rights against employers for breaches of the following Acts.

Equal Pay Act 1970

Health and Safety at Work Act 1974

Sex Discrimination Acts 1975 and 1986

Race Relations Act 1976

Transfer of Undertakings (Protection of Employment) Regulations 1981

Industrial Training Act 1982

Trade Union Reform and Employment Rights Act 1993

Disability Discrimination Act 1995

Employment Rights Act 1996

For most purposes the tribunal will be composed of the chairman and two other members. The chairman must be a barrister, advocate or solicitor of at least seven years' standing, and the other two members who are appointed by the Secretary of State for Employment will be drawn from lists proposed by the employers' organisations and employees' organisations. Under new rules brought in with the **Trade Union Reform and Employment Rights Act 1993,** the chairman may sit alone to hear some cases.

Appeals against the decisions of tribunals, on points of law, may be made to the Employment Appeal Tribunal, and from there to the Court of Appeal. The final arbiter on legal matters in the UK is the House of Lords.

All decisions of appeal courts in the UK (ie the Employment Appeal Tribunal and Court of Appeal) on points of law which establish a legal precedent (ie a principle of legal importance) are binding on the lower courts unless and until they are overturned.

Q2.8   Do contracts of employment have to be in writing?

A.   The common law of contract does not require contracts, including employment contracts, to be in writing. Indeed, many employment contracts, particularly part-time and casual contracts are not in writing — often having been agreed over the telephone.

However, the **Employment Rights Act 1996**, as stated above, does require all regular employees who have worked for at least one month to receive a "written statement" within two months of employment starting.

Q2.9   Does the "written statement of terms and conditions" as required by the Employment Rights Act 1996 constitute a "contract of employment" for legal purposes?

A.   No, because the written statement of terms and conditions as required by the Act only requires certain conditions to be in writing — the total contract of employment may be much more comprehensive.

Q2.10   When does this have to be given?

A.   This has to be given to all employees (other than casual workers) who have worked for one month within two months of starting employment (s.2 **Employment Rights Act 1996**).

A written statement does not have to be given to an employee if:

- the employment lasts for less than one month
- the employment contract lasts for less than eight hours a week
- the employee is employed mainly outside the UK
- the employee is a seaman.

Q2.11   Am I free to negotiate any conditions into a contract?

A.   Under contract law it is normally allowed for the offeror (the person making the contract, eg the employer) to incorporate any conditions he or she wishes — it is for the offeree (the person receiving the offer) to decide whether to accept or not. Once an offer has been accepted the contract becomes binding and can only be altered by mutual agreement, which effectively constitutes a new offer and acceptance.

There are certain terms which may be included into contracts which may be void in law. Many contracts with restrictive covenants, eg restrictions on the future employment of existing employees (eg not to compete) have been held to be void. (*Cantor Fitzgerald (UK) Ltd v Wallace* 1992 IRLR 215.)

Contracts which are intended to break the law are not enforceable, so an agreement to pay part of a wage in cash in order to evade tax and National Insurance liabilities cannot be enforced.

In some cases also, it is not possible to contract to remove or reduce an employee's statutory or common law rights, eg length of notice or health and safety rights.

Q2.12   What has to be specified in a "written statement" as required by the Employment Rights Act 1996?

A.   The **Employment Rights Act 1996** specifies that the following items have to be included in the written statement.

The Principal Statement

Details to be provided in the principal statement are:

(a)   the names of the employer and employee

(b)   the date when employment began

(c)   the date on which the employee's period of continuous employment began (taking into account any employment with a previous employer which counts)

(d) the scale or rate of pay, or the way pay is worked out

(e) the pay intervals (hourly, weekly, monthly, etc)

(f) any terms and conditions relating to hours of work (including normal working hours)

(g) any terms and conditions relating to holiday entitlement including public holidays and holiday pay (including rules on entitlement to accrued holiday pay on termination of employment; these rules must be sufficiently specific to allow the entitlement to be precisely calculated)

(h) job title or a brief job description

(i) place of work, or, if the employee is required or permitted to work at various places, an indication of that fact and the employer's address.

Further Information

The employer must also provide the following within the two month period (either in further instalments or with the principal statement):

(a) any terms and conditions relating to sickness/injury, including sick pay

(b) rules on pension and pension schemes*

(c) length of notice to be given by both employer and employee

(d) if the contract is "temporary", an indication of the expected duration, or the end date of a fixed-term contract

(e) particulars of any collective agreements which directly affect the terms and conditions of the employment including, where the employer is not a party, the persons by whom they were made

(f) where the employee is required to work outside the UK for a period of more than one month; details of the length of posting, the currency in which payment will be made, details of any additional benefits arising from the posting, and any terms and conditions relating to the employee's return to the UK**.

*Note**: This requirement does not apply where the employee's pension rights derive from a statutory scheme under which the employer is already required to provide such information.

****Note**: If the employee is to begin work outside the UK within two months of starting, all the particulars must be given before the employee leaves.

Note on Discipline and Grievance

The statement must also include details of:

(a)   any disciplinary rules applicable

(b)   the name (or description) of the person to whom an employee can apply if dissatisfied with a disciplinary decision, and the manner in which such applications can be made

(c)   the name or description of the person with whom the employee can raise a grievance and the manner in which such applications should be made, and

(d)   an explanation of any additional steps in the disciplinary or grievance procedures.

Note: The ACAS Code of Practice on Discipline recommends that employers have clearly stated disciplinary rules which all employees know and that a person to whom an employee can appeal against a disciplinary decision is someone more senior than the person who made the decision.

An employer who has fewer than 20 employees (including those of associated employers) on the date an employee's continuous service began is not required to supply particulars of disciplinary rules or the procedure to that employee (although the employer must still provide details of how to pursue a grievance).

Details of disciplinary or grievance procedures relating to health or safety at work do not have to be included.

Mandatory Headings in the Statement

The written statement must include the headings listed above: where the employer does not provide the benefit/entitlement in question the statement must say so.

Obligation to Leavers

The employer must still give a written statement to an employee who leaves, or is dismissed, before the two month period for giving the statement has expired.

Reference to Other Documents

The written statement can refer employees to another document for particulars on sickness, pensions, disciplinary rules and the additional (or appeal) steps in the disciplinary or grievance procedure. However, a cross-reference is only permitted where employees have a reasonable opportunity to read the reference document in the course of their employment or where the document is made reasonably accessible in some other way (such as where every employee is provided with a staff handbook).

In addition, the employer can refer the employee to the statutory provisions or a collective agreement on length of notice periods (although, as above, the reference document must be readily accessible to employees).

Changes to Particulars

An employer must give employees individual written notification of any changes to the particulars. The statement must be given at the earliest oportunity, and in any event no later than a month after the change. Details of the change must be given in full although the statement may refer the employee to another document (if it is reasonably accessible) for details of changes to sickness, pensions, additional steps in the disciplinary procedure or notice where cross-references are permitted (see above on reference documents).

Where the change results from the employee being required to work outside the UK for more than a month, then the employee must receive the statement before he or she leaves.

Employer's Name Altered/New Employer

If the employer's name is altered but there is no change in identity or, if there is a change of identity of employer, but this does not cause a break in the employee's period of employment, a fresh statement does not have to be issued if no other terms of employment are changed. However, the employee must be notified in writing of (a) the new name of the employer and (b) the date on which the continuous period of employment began within one month (as above). This involves totalling up all past service that counts as continuous with the former employer or under the same employers' old name and putting this in writing for each individual employee.

Note: The Transfer of Undertakings Regulations 1981 are likely to apply where there is a change in the identity of the employer, for example after the sale of a business.

Excluded Employees

An employer is not required to give a written statement of particulars to an employee if:

(a)   the employment continues for less than a month, or

(b)   the employee is engaged in work wholly or mainly outside Great Britain, or

(c)   the employee is a seaman in a ship registered in the UK under an approved crew agreement.

Where an excluded employee subsequently becomes eligible for a written statement then the two month time limit for providing the statement begins when the employee becomes eligible. However, the employer must still specify in the written statement the actual start date of employment and start date of continuous service.

Complaint to Tribunal

Any employee who has not been given a statement or been informed of changes within the time limits or who thinks a statement given is incorrect or incomplete may complain to an Employment Tribunal within three months of the employer's failure.

The tribunal may then confirm the particulars as they stand or may amend the particulars or may substitute other particulars as it thinks appropriate. The original statement given by the employer is then deemed automatically to include the tribunal's alterations. There is no fine or award of compensation for failing to give a statement or for giving an incorrect or incomplete statement.

Contracts of Employment

A contract of employment comes into effect automatically as soon as a job has been offered and accepted; the terms of the contract are those stated at the interview, or subsequently set out in the letter offering or confirming the job. It is important that these terms are a true representation of the contract, otherwise the new employee could make a claim for damages in court under the **Misrepresentation Act 1967**. Terms might also be implied into the contract by custom and practice or by common law, (eg the duty of good faith or the duty to maintain the employment relationship).

GUARANTEE PAYMENTS

The **Employment Rights Act 1996** provides that employees with at least one month's service must be paid a "guarantee payment" for each workless day, for up to five days in any three month period.

The "workless days" that qualify for this payment are days when an employee is not provided with work by his or her employer because of either:

(i)   a diminution in the employer's business for work of the kind the employee is employed to do, or

(ii)   any other occurrence affecting the normal working of the employer's business in relation to work of the kind which the employee is employed to do.

The right to a guarantee payment is lost if:

(a)   the failure to provide work is a consequence of a trade dispute involving any employee or his or her employer or of an associated employer, or

(b)   the employer has offered the employee suitable alternative employment for the day which has been unreasonably refused, or

(c)   the employee does not comply with reasonable requirements imposed by his or her employer with a view to ensuring that his or her services are available.

So, for instance, lack of work caused by a power workers' strike would qualify for a guarantee payment, but the entitlement would be lost if the workless day was in consequence of a strike by, say, kitchen staff. Similarly, the right would be lost if the reason for lack of work was late delivery of essential goods and the employer had asked employees to remain in the building for an hour or so in the hope that the goods would be received but they had refused to stay.

Further limitations on the right to a guarantee payment are that it is payable only for days when no work at all is carried out. So if workers were sent home after working for two hours, they would not be entitled to a guarantee payment under the legislation, and the right to payment only applies in respect of a day on which the employee would normally be obliged to work in accordance with his or her contract of employment. Therefore, if a business always closes down for a two week period each year, and that fact is included in employment contracts, those two weeks would not qualify employees for guarantee payments even though no work was provided.

The amount of the payment is currently £15.35 (1999/2000) per day (unless this is more than normal earnings, when that figure would apply) and the employee is entitled to be paid for the number of days in his or her normal working week subject to a maximum of five days in any three month period. Thus those working a four-day week will have an entitlement to four days in a three month period but workers on a six-day week will have five days.

To assess whether workers do have an entitlement, it is necessary to look back over the period of three months immediately preceding the workless day and count the number of days when a guarantee payment has been made.

Note: The right for employees to be paid guarantee payments does not entitle the employer to lay them off, unless this is provided for in the contract of employment, as the employer would, in most cases,be in breach of contract even though it paid the guarantee payment, as this will normally be less than the employee's normal daily pay. Such a breach would entitle an employee to leave, without giving notice, and claim unfair constructive dismissal.

Q2.13 Can other documents be incorporated into a contract?

A. Yes. It is quite in order to incorporate other documents into contracts. These can include "house rules", operational manuals, company induction booklets, etc. However, these cannot contain substantial conditions or changes to conditions which were not communicated before employment started.

All major terms of a contract have to be incorporated into the offer at the time it is made.

Q2.14   Does the law specify any minimum or maximum conditions in employment contracts such as pay, hours of work, holidays, sick pay, etc?

A.   Minimum wages and maximum working hours have recently been introduced into the employment law of the UK. Whilst employers can exceed this, it is illegal to pay below the minimum wage. It is not permitted to ask workers to work over the maximum hours unless agreed otherwise.

            There are, of course, statutory sick pay and maternity pay schemes, both of which are covered later in this book. (See also Q3.2.)

Q2.15   How can I change the conditions of employment of my employees?

A.   As written above, once a contract has been made it is, in principle, not possible to modify it except by mutual consent. In fact, a new offer has to be made and accepted. It is possible to include a "unilateral variation" clause. But any variation made under such a clause would have to be reasonable in the circumstances, eg unless a relocation clause was also written in, it is unlikely that to transfer an employee from one country to another under a "unilateral variation" clause would be upheld in court.

            If an employer wishes to change a contract and the employee refuses the proposed change, the employer can terminate the contract and offer a new one on the required terms. If the employee does not wish to accept the new terms, he or she could possibly claim unfair dismissal or constructive dismissal and also sue for breach of contract.

            In terminating one contract and offering another it is vital that the termination and new offer are made clear (*Burdett-Coutts and others v Hertfordshire County Council* (1984 IRLR 91).

Q2.16 **If I change my employees' conditions do I have to issue a new contract?**

A.   The answer to this question falls into two parts. Under common law there is no requirement to make or alter contracts in writing, unless such a condition is written into the original contract. However, it is good business practice to confirm all contracts in writing so that there is less room for misunderstanding should any disagreement arise.

Under the **Employment Rights Act 1996** (s.4) an employer must give employees individual written notification of any changes to contracts within one month of the change taking effect. Details of the change must be given in full although the statement may refer the employee to other documents. Where an employer changes or the employer changes name the employee must be notified in writing of the new name of the employer and the date when continuous employment began.

Q2.17 **If I forget to insert certain clauses into a contract, what can I do to rectify the situation?**

A.   The answer to this question is basically the same as the answer to Q2.15. In essence you have to make a new offer and obtain acceptance of the new offer.

Q2.18 **If I discover that an employee gave me false or misleading information in his or her application, can I dismiss that person?**

A.   Under the **Misrepresentation Act 1967** "where a person enters into a contract after a misrepresentation, and that misrepresentation has become a term of the contract, or the contract has been formed, then he will be able to rescind the contract" (s.1 **Misrepresentation Act 1967**).

From this it is apparent that if an applicant for a position claims qualifications or experience which he or she does not have then the employer may have the right to rescind the contract. In practice, many employees will exagerate their claims to skills or experience and so employers would have to decide if the misrepresentation is fundamental or merely a "slight change of emphasis". If, for example, an applicant for a head chef's position claimed to have controlled a brigade of 20 but had never controlled more than five, this might be deemed to be a misrepresentation.

Q2.19 **What happens if an employer misrepresents a job?**

A. If an employer misrepresents a job then the employee can rescind the contract and could also sue for damages (*McNally n Welltrade International, T James and Welltrade Middle East Ltd* 1978 IRLR 497).

Q2.20 **If I receive a very adverse reference about a newly employed member of staff, what can I do?**

A. Often an offer of employment is made subject to certain conditions, such as the achievement of a qualification or the receipt of satisfactory references. It is quite in order for an employer to make a "conditional offer" so long as the condition is made absolutely clear. If the condition cannot be complied with there is no offer outstanding to be accepted.

If the employee has already started employment, basically the same principle applies, and as the employee has to be employed for two years to qualify for "unfair dismissal" protection (**Employment Rights Act 1996** s.108) the employer might rescind the contract without fear of the employee taking the case to an Employment Tribunal (unless the employee chooses to use reasons such as racial, sex, disability or trade union discrimination or the **Rehabilitation of Offenders Act**, as a reason).

Q2.21 **Can conditions be implied into contracts of employment by anyone who is not party to the contract?**

A. Yes. The courts can address problems in an employment relationship. One example concerned a woman who worked for a firm of solictors. In her work area there were several smokers and she asked her employers to provide her with a smoke-free work area. The employers did not. The woman resigned and then started "constructive dismissal" proceedings. An Employment Tribunal and the Employment Appeal Tribunal found in her favour (*Waltons & Morse v Dorrington* [1997] IRLR488).

3. PAY AND BENEFITS

Q3.1 **What exactly is meant by the term "wages" in terms of the specific elements included?**

A.   The **Wages Act 1986**, consolidated within the **Employment Rights Act 1996**, modernised the law in terms of the payment of wages and salaries. Under the Act, "wages" is deemed to mean any sums payable to the employee by the employer in connection with that employment. It includes any fee, bonus, commission, holiday pay or other emolument relevant to the employment, whether specified in the contract of employment or not (*Kent Management Services Ltd. v Butterfield* (1992) ICR 272). Wages also includes Statutory Sick Pay (SSP) and Statutory Maternity Pay (SMP), guarantee payments, payment for time off for union duties, payment for time off for ante-natal care, and payment while under medical suspension.

Wages do not include the repayment of expenses, any advance on wages, any compensation or severance pay and any redundancy pay. Payments in kind are normally excluded from the definition of wages except items like luncheon vouchers, which are transferrable into a fixed monetary value. Payments in lieu of notice are not wages, as these are paid after the termination of the contract, in effect to compensate for breach of the contract to provide work (*Delaney v Staples* (1992) ICR 483). When considering compensation at an Employment Tribunal, a week's pay is taken as the gross pay under the contract, or the average of the last 12 weeks' pay if piece rate or commission applies (*Cooner v PS Doal & Son* (1988) IRLR 338 EAT).

Q3.2 **What are the key facts about the recently announced National Minimum Wage (NMW)?**

A.   Following the Low Pay Commission's report to the Prime Minister, and the ongoing subsequent consultation, the current situation on the NMW can be summarised as follows.

1.   A National Minimum Wage (NMW) will be set at £3.60 per hour for those over 21 years of age, effective from April 1999, rising to £3.70 in June 2000.

2.   A Development Rate will operate for those aged 18 to 21 and those on accredited training schemes, set at £3.00 per hour from April 1999, rising to £3.20 per hour in June 2000.

3.   Those aged 16 and 17 years old and those on apprentice-ships will be excluded from the NMW.

4.   Employers will need to include full NMW details on payslips, display details prominently in the workplace, and will face severe penalties for not complying with the NMW law to be introduced. (Enforcement will be via the Contributions Agency).

The NMW will be defined as follows.

1.   The NMW will apply to gross earnings before tax, NIC and other authorised deductions.

2.   Incentive payments should count towards the NMW in the pay period in which they are received rather than earned.

3.   Any service charge payment or tips paid centrally through the payroll must be included in the calculation of the NMW.

4.   Cash tips and gratuities paid directly by the customer to an employee are not included in the NMW computations.

5.   Payments for overtime, special allowances and shift supple-ments are not included.

6.   Benefits are not included, with the important exception within the hospitality industry, of accommodation, where an offset of up to a maximum of £20 per week may be allowed.

7.   In calculating the NMW, earnings should be averaged over a normal pay period of up to a maximum of one month.

8.   The NMW should apply to all working time when a worker is required to be at the place of work and be available for such work.

Copies of the Low Pay Commission's Report may be obtained from the DTI Publications Orderline, tel: 0870 1502 500.

Q3.3   **What must I include in an itemised pay statement?**

A.   Under the **Employment Rights Act 1996**, an employee must be given, on or before pay day, an itemised pay statement containing the following details:

- gross amount of wages or salary
- net amount of wages or salary
- variable deductions and the purposes for which they are made
- fixed deductions and the purposes for which they are made
- where different parts of the net amount are paid in different ways, the amount and method of payment for each part payment
- if a company operates an Inland Revenue approved profit related pay (PRP) scheme, the payslip must show PRP separate from gross pay.

This requirement applies to all employees regardless of hours worked.

The statement of fixed deductions does not have to be given each time if, instead, employees have been given a standing statement of such fixed deductions. This standing statement must be updated every 12 months. The easier it is to understand the pay statement, the less confusion and fewer problems there are likely to be.

Q3.4   **Am I obliged to provide holiday pay?**

A.   On 1 October 1998, the Working Time Directive came into force. Apart from the more publicised elements regarding a maximum working week of 48 hours, this Directive also sets minimum annual paid leave entitlement at three weeks, rising to four weeks in November 1999, held over for three months for new employees. This means that employers will have to pay cash in lieu to employees who terminate after only three months, increasing the holiday pay burden quite considerably in an industry with many short-term workers. These provisions regarding annual paid leave will be enforced by the Employment Tribunals.

Public holidays — there is no statutory right to public holidays (paid or unpaid) such as Good Friday, so public holidays could be counted in the statutory annual allowance.

Q3.5 **How do I handle holiday pay and entitlement in a business which closes down in the winter months?**

A. Within any statement of terms and conditions, information on holidays should be stated precisely, so that the employee is fully aware of his or her entitlement to holidays, holiday pay, and accrued holiday pay on termination of employment. If there are special business needs regarding when employees may take their holidays, this needs to be included in the written statement of terms and conditions of employment. For example, a seasonal hotel may include in its written terms that all paid holiday must be taken at the end of the trading season, when the business closes. It is common for such businesses to put limits on the amount of holiday that can be taken at any particular time, or to employ staff only on fixed-term contracts for the season, with the understanding of minimal holiday entitlement, and the payment of accrued holiday pay on completion of the contract.

Q3.6 **What rights do I have regarding the board and lodging which I provide for my live-in staff?**

A. Such provision must be clearly spelt out in written terms, most appropriately in the form of a licence which can be terminated upon termination of employment. The provisions of this arrangement should specify that the employee is responsible for maintaining the fixtures and fittings in the condition and standard existing when taking up the accommodation (given normal wear and tear), when a detailed inventory of contents and description of their condition should be undertaken. The penalties for damage must be clearly communicated in both disciplinary and financial terms. The arrangements for inspection of the room should also be clarified. Above all, it must be understood that when the employee leaves his or her employment, on the effective date of termination, he or she must vacate the premises.

The termination of an employee's licence to occupy residential accommodation provided by the employer does not have to comply with the notice provisions of the **Protection from Eviction Act 1977**.

On the financial side, note that the provision of free board and lodging with a consequent reduction in pay is not within the scope of the National Insurance Contribution (NIC) definition of earnings with consequent savings for employer and employee. However, if the employee is paid a gross wage out of which a rental or deduction is made, then the employee is liable to be taxed on the whole salary. It should also be noted that within the recent National Minimum Wage (NMW) proposals, the benefit of accommodation may be included in NMW calculations up to a maximum of £20 per week.

Q3.7   How do I recover overpayments of wages?

A.   The **Employment Rights Act 1996** s.14 has simplified the permission to deduct for overpayment. However, the circumstances of the overpayment must be examined. The defence is really that the employer has led the employee to believe that he or she is entitled to the payment (*Avon County Council v Howlett* (1983) IRLR 171). A more recent case indicates that the appropriate defence is that the employee has in good faith changed his or her financial position as a result of the overpayment, so that it would be inequitable to order recovery of the overpayment, although any amount not yet spent may be recovered (*Lipkin Gorman v Karpnale Ltd* (1992) 4 All ER 512)). If it could be proved that the employee had realised the mistake before spending the money, failure to return the overpayment could lead to a prosecution under the **Theft Act 1968**. It is advisable to provide in the written statement of terms and conditions of employment that any overpayment, whether from mistake of fact or law, can be recovered from an employee by deduction from wages due. This cannot lead to a breach of the **Wages Act 1986**.

Q3.8   What deductions from wages are authorised by law?

A.   The **Employment Rights Act 1996** provides clear deduction rules for employers. Under these rules, employers must not make deductions from a worker's pay unless that deduction is required by statute, or it is authorised by a term of the contract of employment which has been notified in writing to the employee, or the employee has agreed in writing to the deduction. (Deduction also covers payments from the employee to the employer, eg loans repayments).

The normal statutory, authorised deductions are namely PAYE tax and National Insurance Contributions (NIC). Any other deduction must be agreed beforehand by the employee, whether as part of an agreed and signed contract of employment or in some other written form. The worker's agreement to the deduction must pre-date the actual deduction (*Discount Tobacco & Confectionery Ltd v Williamson* (1993) ICR 371). Other exceptions can be the recovery of an overpayment of wages or expenses, the result of statutory disciplinary procedings, because the employee has taken part in a strike or other industrial action and has therefore refused to work, or to satisfy a court order or employment tribunal decision (although even here the worker's consent should be obtained in writing). Other authorised deductions include Attachment of Earnings orders and Child Support Agency orders.

Q3.9   How can I get all my employees to be paid through a bank account?

A.   The **Wages Act 1986** repealed the Truck Acts of 1831 and 1860, which imposed restrictions on the method of payment of wages, in particular that manual workers were to be paid in "coin of the realm". Therefore the statutory right to insist on payment in cash no longer exists. However, the method of paying wages now really rests as a matter for agreement between the employer and the employee. The basic fact though is that those employees who were paid in cash before the Truck Acts were repealed (with effect from 1 January 1987), cannot be compelled to change to cheque or credit transfer through a bank account. If you are determined to impose such a new payment system, then ultimately you would have to terminate the old contract of employment and offer a new one. More appropriately, it is best to consult with staff and try to persuade them that the new method is better for all concerned and obtain their written consent to such a change. If you also intend to change the frequency of payment from weekly to monthly, then you will need to provide contingency plans for your employees in order for them to be able to change their budgeting cycle. This is normally done through a system of decreasing advances on wages over a fixed period. If difficulty is experienced in getting agreement to change to direct transfer, it is normal to offer an incentive in terms of a one-off cash payment.

Q3.10   How can I recover cash shortages after my employees have been incompetent in cash handling?

A.   Apart from the deductions discussed in Q3.8, there are some special rules under the **Employment Rights Act 1996** (s.17–22) for those employees within retail employment, including hotel and catering workers who are cash handlers or are responsible for controlling stock.

1. The employer must notify the employee of the total amount of the deduction to be made in respect of deficiencies of cash or shortages of stock and then issue a demand in writing and on pay-day.

2. Where losses are attributable, then deductions are limited to one tenth of gross wages on any particular pay day.

3. If this deduction does not cover the entire deficiency, further deductions may be made as long as no more than one tenth of gross wages is deducted at any one time.

4. Deductions must be made within 12 months of the discovery of the shortage, and if the employee leaves, there is no limit as to the amount that can be deducted from the final pay packet, as long as it is within the 12 month period.

Q3.11 What happens regarding the payment of staff if the business fails?

A. Employees do have certain protection under the **Insolvency Act 1986,** whereby their remuneration is given a degree of preferential debt provision, that up to four months' wages can be recovered. There is an upper limit on the amount which is altered from time to time. The remuneration includes all the normal elements of "wages", but it does not include any award for unfair dismissal, nor for any notice period money that might be due after insolvency. The employee may be able to recover further sums from the Department for Education and Employment, such as arrears of pay and accrued holiday pay, but only to a total sum of £220 per week.

Q3.12 How do I handle the equal pay issue when I have many different types of employees and lengths of service?

A. In basic terms the **Equal Pay Act 1970** gave men and women the right to equal pay, where they were doing like work, or work rated as equivalent or work of equal value. To claim unfair treatment at an Employment Tribunal, the man or woman must identify a comparator colleague, whether a current worker or perhaps a predecessor (*Hayward v Cammell Laird* (1988) House of Lords IRLR 257). To avoid a claim, the most systematic and expensive approach would be to undertake a full job evaluation exercise but this may be impractical. You must be sure of your job categories within the organisation chart and of the specific responsibilities and accountabilities of the various positions. You should also look across departments for comparators as the responsibilities of a particular grade of chef might be deemed as of equal value to a particular grade of receptionist. There are of course good reasons why some people in jobs of equal value might be paid at different levels, namely experience, qualifications, individual merit and length of service. However, you must be sure that these legitimate differences do exist between job-holders of different gender.

It is not, for example, sufficient to give people different job titles which really mean very little in terms of responsibility, as in a case where a waitress was paid less than a male comparator who was given the title of "banqueting supervisor" (*Sorbie v Trust House Forte Hotels Ltd* (1977)ITR 85 EAT). However, in another case where equal value was claimed, it was clearly shown that a male canteen worker was not comparable to a female colleague, because he was required to work shifts, be responsible for stock control and handle money, none of which the female undertook (*Capper Pass Ltd v Allan* (1980)ICR 434 HL). In a case which reached the House of Lords, North Yorkshire County Council was found to have breached the equal pay legislation when it cut the pay of dinner ladies following privatisation of the school meals service. The ladies were able to show that they were then paid less than the male workers who had previously been the comparators for assessing work of equal value.

Q3.13 What elements of remuneration are counted when carrying out an analysis for equal pay purposes?

A. For the purposes of wage calculation and comparability, the **Equal Pay Act 1970** defines pay in Article 119 as "basic wage plus any other consideration, either in cash or kind, which the worker receives directly or indirectly in respect of his employment from his employer". Pay therefore includes elements other than basic wage, like bonuses, performance-related pay, individual merit payments, and specific benefits of a particular job, such as company car, health insurance and in-company discounts. There must also be consideration of any occupational pension schemes into which the employer may make contributions for the employee, and is therefore considered as an element of pay.

Q3.14 What arrangements must I undertake regarding the provision of pensions for my employees?

A. Whilst there is universal right to the state pension in the United Kingdom, based upon the individual's contribution record, the right to occupational pension as well is determined by the employer and the written terms and conditions of the employee's contract. The particulars of any pension or pension scheme must be contained within the written statement of terms and conditions of employment, though the full details may be published elsewhere. However, if there are no pension rights, then the contract must clearly state that fact, for failure to do so can lead to problems of implied terms at any future tribunal hearing (*Eagland v British Telecommunications plc* (1992)IRLR 323 CA). Many companies now actively promote an occupational pension scheme having "contracted out" of the second level of state pensions, the State Earnings Related Pension Scheme (SERPS). The SERPS is under review by the present Government. Other recent moves emanate from the **Pensions Act 1995**, fully enforced in April 1997. This legislation has enabled company pension schemes to start at a lower level of contribution in an attempt to make such schemes more attractive to the lower paid. There are also new and more stringent procedures for the proper administration of pension trusts and funds.

Some employers also make contributions on behalf of their employees, whilst others are purely the contribution from the employee who may also make additional voluntary contributions (AVC) to top up the eventual pensionable amount. Where an occupational pension scheme does exist, regulations under the **Social Security Act 1985** insist that full details are available to members, spouses, beneficiaries and any recognised trade unions. It is also now unlawful to exclude part-time employees from an occupational scheme on the basis that to do so would result in sex discrimination as most part-timers are women. Advice on setting up an occupational pension scheme may be sought from the Department for Education and Employment or from professional pension advisors.

Q3.15 **What regulations apply to the receiving of gifts by employees?**

A. This question concerns personal gifts given by the employer to employees. Tips and gratuities clearly fall under the scope of the Inland Revenue, and are normally the personal responsibility of the employee, unless a "tronc" is in operation when the supervisor of the "tronc" is held responsible for declaration of income for tax purposes. In the case of gifts from employer to employee, the original approach was the so-called "convertibilty test" whereby the gift or fringe benefit would only be considered as remuneration and liable to tax if it could be converted into cash. Gifts of £10 and under will not be subject to taxation. Since 1988, there has been a distinction between the gifts received by directors and those earning £8500 per annum or more and those earning less than £8500. For directors and those earning £8500 per annum or more, the tax is calculated on the cost of the benefit to the employer and not, as was effectively the case, the second-hand value. There is a rider that depreciation may be taken into account thus estimating the gift at current market value. For those earning less than £8500 the "convertibility test" still applies and is therefore more favourable (*Wilkins v Rogerson 1961*). Note that anything like a voucher which can be converted into gifts is to be avoided as the full cost will be taxable. Also, if an employer reimburses the employee for prior purchase of a gift, then the full cost of the gift will be taxable.

Q3.16 **Are there any tax implications in respect of benefits and perks received by staff as part of their terms and conditions?**

A.   Yes. Again, the regulations set out in the previous answer apply, and it is the duty of the employer to deduct tax from the employee's earnings for all benefits, including car and fuel allowances for travel to work, meal vouchers, private telephone bills (where use is not exclusively for work), and accommodation except where it is part of the terms and conditions of the job or is a customary provision or for security purposes. The employer may not choose to treat all these types of benefits as PAYE tax deductions, but must in that case complete annually Form P11D for those earning £8500 or more and P9D for those earning under £8500. Beneficial loans at attractive interest rates also come under the P11D umbrella, taxable on a cash equivalence basis amounting to an interest rate of 7.5% (from 6 January 1994). Any interest paid by the employee is deducted from the taxable amount. There are two exemptions, namely small loans where the cash eqivalent does not exceed £5000 in any tax year, and loans for qualifying purposes, of up to the first £30,000 for the purchase of property which is the employee's only or main residence.

Q3.17 **What is the current situation on National Insurance Contributions (NIC's)?**

A.   Employers have a duty to pay National Insurance Contributions (NIC's) in respect of their employees but not in respect of self-employed employees. The current system was established under the **Social Security Contributions and Benefits Act 1992** to provide for sick pay, unemployment benefit, pensions, maternity pay, widowhood and industrial injuries. The level of NIC depends on the wage or salary earned and has lower and upper limits. For the tax year at the time of writing (1999/2000), the lower limit for employees is £66 per week and up to that sum the employee pays 2%, and then 10% between £66 and £500 per week at the upper limit when employee contribution ceases. The employer's rate of contribution depends on whether the business has contracted out of the State Earnings Related Pension Scheme (SERPS). At the time of writing, the maximum for a contracted-out employer is 10.0% on all earnings of £220 per week or more.

Employers' contributions are as follows:

Below £66 per week wage:	Nil
Above £66	12.2%

There is an excellent freephone advisory service on current rates and practice provided by the Contributions Agency (to be merged with the Inland Revenue in the near future) and the number can be found in your local phone book.

Q3.18   Should part-timers be paid on a pro-rata basis with full-time staff?

A.   All the recent legislation in the UK, and rulings from the European Court of Justice have greatly enhanced the standing and employment rights of the ever-increasing number of part-time workers in the labour force (see **Employment Protection (Part-time Employees) Regulations 1995**). In particular, there is the precedent that to treat part-timers differently to full-timers could be construed as sex discrimination against women as the majority of part-timers are female. This has been particularly strengthened by the **Occu-**

pational **Pension Schemes (Equal Access to Membership) Amendment Regulations 1995** which make it unlawful to exclude part-timers from an occupational pension scheme. As a result part-time employees should benefit, pro-rata, from the same terms and conditions as full-timers. There is no justification for paying part-timers less than the basic rate for the job, other than through the normal reasons for differences in pay which do not transgress the equal pay situation, such as length of service and individual merit. However, a recent European Court of Justice ruling on a German case (*Stadt Lengerich v Angelika Helmig* 1995) is clear in confirming that overtime payments need only be at the enhanced rate (eg time and a half) once the hours worked go beyond the normal hours worked by full-time colleagues.

The situation will be further endorsed in 1999 by the enforcement of a European Union Directive on part-time work, as part of the Social Charter. This Directive has a main aim of giving part-time workers the same rights, pro-rata, as their full-time colleagues and to remove discrimination against part-timers in all aspects of employment. It also stresses the need for employees to embrace the more flexible labour market now pertaining in many economies and aims to encourage employers to encourage part-timers and benefit from their flexibility and reliability.

Q3.19 What are the new rules concerning "check-off", the means of employees paying their union subscriptions?

A.   Those in trade unionised sectors of the industry will be pleased to know that the "check-off" system has been simplified under the Deregulation (Deduction from Pay of Union Subscriptions) Order which came into force on 23 June 1998. It will not be necessary to obtain repeat authorisation at least every three years to confirm the employee's desire to pay the union subscriptions direct from wages, and the employer will no longer have to notify the employee at least one month in advance if the amount to be deducted is to rise. Employers must still obtain agreement in writing before the deductions can commence, and the sum must appear on the itemised pay statement. Employees can withdraw from check-off at any time.

Q3.20   What are the main types of Employee Share Option Scheme?

A.   There are three main types of scheme which are approved by the Inland Revenue and attract tax relief: profit-sharing schemes, where all employees get a stake in the company's fortunes and take a share of the hoped-for profits; savings-related share option schemes, where an agreed amount of savings is deducted from salary for a number of years, gains interest in a special account and which can later be used to purchase discounted shares; and all-employee share option schemes, where qualifying employees are offered options worth a percentage of their wage or salary, the profit on the options being paid out in shares at some time in the future. Such schemes have been extremely popular in recent years in order to increase employee commitment, involvement and re-ward. Before setting up such a scheme you must get detailed advice from an expert and from the Inland Revenue and be quite clear as to why you want to introduce such a scheme, which will itself have implications for resources and costs. One well-touted example is that of the supermarket chain Asda, which introduced an employee share option scheme in an attempt to reduce labour turnover. It replaced its previous profit-sharing scheme and any employee with one year's service, working at least 15 hours per week, was offered options worth 25% of annual salary. The profit on half the option (in terms of share price) is paid out after three years, the balance after six years. Leaving too soon means you lose the accrued benefit, and labour turnover has indeed been reduced.

4. SICKNESS

Q4.1 Am I obliged to provide sick pay?

A. Employees are not automatically entitled to sick pay unless the contract of employment specifically states that this benefit is part of the terms and conditions of the employment. Employers are obliged to pay Statutory Sick Pay (SSP) in circumstances outlined later in this section, and where the employee is qualified to receive such payments. In the absence of a clearly defined contractual agreement as to how long the sick pay benefit will last, this will be for a reasonable period only (*Howman & Son v Blyth* (1983) IRLR 139).

Q4.2 What details should I give my staff about sickness schemes?

A. The right of an employee to receive payment when sick depends very much on the terms and conditions of employment. If a company sickness scheme exists, then full particulars must be itemised within the written statement of main terms and conditions (**Employment Rights Act 1996**). If no express term within the contract exists, there is no presumption in favour of payment, and previous custom and practice will be taken into consideration by a court, unless a specific agreement has been entered into (*Mears v Safecar Security Ltd* (1982) IRLR 183).

However, under the Statutory Sick Pay (SSP) scheme, the **Social Security Contributions and Benefits Act 1992** amended the previous 1982 legislation which introduced SSP and placed a clear obligation on all employers to provide such SSP payments in most circumstances for all qualifying employees. The employer may be responsible for up to 28 weeks' SSP in any one period of incapacity for work at the prevailing rates.

It is best practice for an employer to give full details of such schemes in any contract of employment, leaving the employee in no doubt as to their rights. Entitlement should be spelt out by confirming the company scheme procedures and the qualifying rules and procedures for SSP. Regarding company schemes, it is important to inform the employee of the benefit in number of weeks' pay dependent on length of service, the reporting procedure for the employee to follow if sick, and details of the self-certification scheme.

Q4.3   How do I handle Statutory Sick Pay (SSP) arrangements for new and existing employees?

A.   Most employees, including part-timers, are entitled to SSP and there is no minimum service qualification. Non-qualifying employees include those over 65 years or under 16 years of age, those with a contract of employment of less than three calendar months and those pregnant employees from the 11th week before the expected date of birth, and for the following 18 weeks. To qualify for SSP the employee must be incapable of carrying out normal duties and be incapacitated for four or more consecutive working days.

All employees must be given details of SSP, preferably within the written statement of terms and conditions. The following points should be noted.

1.   If an employee was given a form SSP1(L), the "Leavers' Statement", by his or her previous employer, this must be given to the new supervisor or personnel department.

2.   The leavers' statement, which employers must complete on termination of employment of each employee, must show the first day of incapacity for work in the period of incapacity for work (PIW), the number of weeks of SSP payable, and the last day for which SSP was payable.

3.   If a new employee falls sick, the leavers' statement issued by the previous employer must be accepted and received within seven calendar days of the first qualifying day in the PIW.

4. The SSP rate will be in accordance with the current scales and regulations, details of which may be obtained from the Department of Social Security (DSS).

5. Where an employee receives both SSP and company sick pay benefit, the total will not exceed the normal basic wage.

6. If the SSP entitlement is exceeded (beyond 28 weeks), but the employee still qualifies for company benefit, he or she will be asked to declare the amount received from the DSS, and this will be deducted from his or her wage. The employer must complete form SSP1 for the employee.

Q4.4   What is a period of incapacity for work (PIW)?

A.   Statutory Sick Pay (SSP) is not payable unless the employee has been absent from work through illness for at least four complete days, whether or not they were all working days, and where the worker is incapable of carrying out their normal duties due to physical or mental sickness or disablement. Such periods of incapacity for work (PIWs) may be consolidated into one period only if separated by no more than 56 days.

Q4.5   What governs the payment rate of Statutory Sick Pay (SSP)?

A.   The rate of SSP depends on the employees' gross average weekly earnings during the eight weeks preceding the period of incapacity for work (PIW). With effect from 6 April 1998 the new SSP rate was fixed at £57.70 per week where gross weekly average earnings are £64 or more. No SSP is payable to those below £64, the so-called lower earnings limit. The maximum entitlement is thus 28 weeks at £57.70, totalling £1,615.60. SSP payments are to be made on the normal pay day or the next following day.

Q4.6   How can I recover Statutory Sick Pay (SSP)?

A.   Since 6 April 1995, an SSP compensation scheme has been in operation known as the Percentage Threshold Scheme (PTS), aiming to assist all employers facing exceptionally high levels of sickness absence. The PTS provides for full reimbursement of an employer's costs paid in any month where these exceed 13% of the gross National Insurance Contribution (NIC) for that month. Monthly calculations need to be made to see if the SSP is recoverable, by assessing the gross NIC's for the tax month, the employees' primary and the employers' secondary contributions (excluding any Class 1A liabilities), multiplying the figure by 13% and calculating the total SSP paid in the month. For example:

Class 1 NIC liability for month:	£420.00
The 13% PTS amount:	54.60
SSP paid in month:	80.00
Recoverable amount:	25.40

SSP details need to be entered on the tax form P14 and the year end form P35 where recovery was made under the PTS.

Q4.7   How do I actually reclaim Statutory Sick Pay (SSP)?

A.   The amount of SSP paid which can be reclaimed should be deducted from the total sum of the employees' and employer's Class 1 NIC's for the tax month in which SSP is paid. If the amount of SSP exceeds the NIC's due, the excess may be deducted from the PAYE income tax due that month. When filling in the PAYE payslip (form P30B(2)) the procedure is to enter the actual net amount of NIC's being paid, ie the contribution less any SSP being reclaimed. Where the SSP is greater than the NIC's, the excess is entered in the box as a minus figure, and deducted from the PAYE amount.

Q4.8   What action should I take in the case of an employee who has been absent through sickness on a long-term basis?

A.   If the sickness or injury is so serious that the carrying out of normal duties is impossible, then a frustration of contract may apply, such as where an employee is disqualified from driving when that very task is the purpose of the job (*Williams v Watsons Luxury Coaches Ltd* (1990) IRLR 164 EAT).

However, for most cases it is a more delicate matter of whether the job can be kept open for someone with a long-term illness. For many small businesses this could be a crucial issue. The employer must take into consideration the status, capability and length of service of the individual and the possibility of alternative employment, but may only contact the employee's doctor if the employee gives written consent (**Access to Medical Reports Act 1988**).

Close contact must be maintained with the individual, and if dismissal is likely to be the only outcome, then a period of meaningful consultation and warning of the possible outcome must take place. Whether company scheme or SSP (for which the limit is 28 weeks), sickness benefit schemes must be followed. Proper notice of termination, if finally necessary under the terms and conditions of the contract of employment, must be given.

Q4.9 **What are the guidelines for a self-certification procedure on sickness?**

A.   Since June 1982 a self-certification scheme has been in operation, whereby doctors do not issue medical certificates for up to and including seven days' absence from work. Most companies have therefore introduced a self-certification procedure, which takes the form of a company benefits claim. Following a period of sickness absence, the employee must complete a self-certification form on his or her return to work. The form must include full details of the absence, confirmation by the supervisor, and the employee must give details of the illness. Longer periods of sickness must be supported by a medical certificate and the employee must only return to work when signed off by the doctor, thus confirming that the employee is fit to return. Employers can insist on a doctor's medical certificate from the first day of absence through sickness if it is felt that an employee is abusing the system.

Q4.10 **What measures do I take against an employee who has regular single days' absence from duty?**

A. The hospitality industry has traditionally suffered from a high level of absenteeism, very often of short duration, and perhaps caused by the pressures and lifestyle of many catering workers. Such absences, even if only for one day, must be formally recorded, and any regularity or pattern identified. The self-certification process must be enforced rigorously and be seen to be taken very seriously, and if problems do arise, it is best to approach the individual and, where appropriate, their supervisor to express concern over the health and absence record of the individual. The spirit of any counselling discussions must be positive and constructive. It is often of value to agree with the employee some form of joint action, such as a commitment to a proper medical check-up or a review of their satisfaction with the job and its environment. In certain cases, resort to disciplinary action may be necessary, such as giving a warning about the amount and pattern of sick leave and stating the consequences of future problems, and what behaviour is expected and acceptable.

5. MATERNITY ISSUES

Q5.1   **What time off for antenatal care must I give a pregnant employee?**

A.   All pregnant employees, regardless of length of service or hours of work per week, are entitled to reasonable time off work for antenatal care, as set out in the **Employment Act 1980** and reiterated in the **Employment Rights Act 1996**. It is important to note that antenatal care must be distinguished from sickness during pregnancy, and is concerned with the woman's appointments at a hospital or clinic prior to the birth. These usually begin between the 8th and 12th week of pregnancy and thereafter at monthly intervals, although clearly depend on the particular health circumstances of each woman. Towards the last two months of pregnancy, the frequency of visits to a clinic may well increase to one every two weeks. The employee should request the time off, but not be refused unreasonably. There is also precedence to include relaxation and parentcraft classes under the banner of antenatal care, if recommended by a registered medical advisor (*Gregory v Tudsbury* (1982) IRLR 267).

A pregnant woman has the right to take time off, paid at the normal hourly rate during normal working hours, and Employment Tribunals invariably find in favour of the employee if the employer feels the employee is being unreasonable about the incidence and timing of appointments, especially if medical advisors have recommended such visits (*Edgar v Georgione Inns Ltd* COIT 1803/13). It is unlawful to dismiss an employee or select for redundancy an employee solely or mainly due to the fact that she has sought to invoke her statutory right to paid time off work for antenatal care.

Except in the case of her first appointment, the employee must be prepared to show her employer on request either a certificate of pregnancy (MATB1) from a registered medical practitioner, midwife or health visitor, or an appointment card or similar document which clearly shows that an appointment has been made.

Q5.2   What is the current situation on maternity leave?

A.   Since the EC Pregnant Workers Directive came into effect in October 1994, all pregnant workers, regardless of length of service or hours of service per week, are entitled to 14 weeks' statutory maternity leave, commencing at any point during the 11 weeks prior to the expected date of childbirth.

During this short-term period of maternity leave, all contractual rights must be maintained except normal wages, for example holiday entitlement, company benefits and pension scheme contributions by the employer. A further right is that if a redundancy situation arises during the maternity leave, the employee must be offered a suitable alternative vacancy if one is available. The employer must pay Statutory Maternity Pay (SMP) to qualifying employees. The leave may be extended due to certified medical reasons, or if the baby is born late. The new legislation gives all women, regardless of length of service, the right not to be dismissed on purely maternity-related grounds, with the exception of a case of legitimate redundancy.

The employee must give at least 21 days' notice of her intention to commence maternity leave, except where premature birth renders this impossible, and she must produce a certificate of pregnancy (MATB1) from a doctor or midwife. If the employee becomes absent from work on pregnancy-related grounds after the 6th week before the expected date of childbirth, the employer can insist that the period of maternity leave commences from the date of absence.

Employees who have completed two years' continuous service are entitled to the longer additional period of maternity absence, which begins at the end of the maternity leave up to the end of the 28th week after the week in which the baby is born. Contractual benefits during this additional maternity absence should be agreed formally between the employer and employee.

It is most important that employers follow the procedures carefully and with due care and consideration, as tribunals consider the onus of proper conduct lies with the employer (*Hilton International Hotels (UK) Ltd v Kaissi* (1994) IRLR 270).

Q5.3 **What happens to a woman's terms and conditions when she is on maternity leave?**

A. An employee on maternity leave (the 14 week period) has a statutory right to continue to benefit from all her terms and conditions except normal salary/wages. She must be considered otherwise to remain in employment, and her length of service is unbroken. For example, she must continue to benefit from contractual aspects such as:

- accrued holiday entitlement
- employers' occupational pension scheme contributions
- company car
- mobile phone (unless provided only for business usage)
- share option schemes
- reimbursement of professional subscriptions
- contractual perks such as health club membership.

Women on full maternity absence have no statutory right to a continuation of employment rights, and this period very much depends on the agreement between the parties. In most cases the relationship continues as employment, with the P45 being retained by the employer and the employee remaining on the payroll being clear indicators. A detailed agreement should be drawn up regarding all contractual rights and benefits during the maternity absence, and employers must be extremely careful not to act against either equal pay or sex discrimination legislation.

Q5.4   What are the notification requirements connected to maternity leave?

A.   To exercise the right to maternity leave and Statutory Maternity Pay (SMP), the employee must produce the medical certificate which confirms the expected date of birth, and should indicate whether she intends to return to work, especially after the longer period of maternity absence. She must also indicate the date on which she intends to commence the maternity leave and/or the receipt of SMP. These matters must be notified at least 21 days in advance of beginning maternity leave. If the birth occurs before the notified date, or even before such a date has been given, the employee is required as soon as is reasonably practicable to inform the employer of the date of birth. Maternity leave would start automatically on the date of birth in such circumstances.

If the employee is absent due to pregnancy-related causes (notified to the employer as soon as possible) before either notification or the notified date, maternity leave commences automatically on the first day of absence after the beginning of the 6th week before the expected week of childbirth. If absent through an illness unconnected with the pregnancy, the employee may take normal sick leave and sick pay/SSP until the maternity leave begins, which will be on the previously notified date.

Q5.5   Is an employee automatically entitled to return to work after maternity leave/absence?

A.   An employee entitled to maternity leave of 14 weeks, or an employee with two years' service entitled to additional maternity absence from the end of the maternity leave to the end of the 28th week after the week of childbirth, has a right to return to work after that period to the same job and terms and conditions, provided that when giving 21 days' notice of her intention to start maternity leave, she stated her intention to return. If, on account of redundancy, she cannot return to her old job, she must be offered a suitable alternative position if one is available, on terms and conditions not substantially less favourable. If the redundancy is legitimate, the employee would be entitled to full redundancy pay, with the maternity leave counting as service. She must still give the employer notification that she intends to return to work and, at least 21 days beforehand, notify of her proposed date of return.

The return to work after maternity absence may be postponed by the employee by up to four weeks on medical certification, and the employer may postpone her return by up to four weeks also, due to specified reasons. The reasons must be notified to the employee, and may be due to the general business requirements of the employer and not necessarily limited to the circumstances connected with the maternity absence. Any extension of the four week period must be by agreement between employer and employee, otherwise a dismissal may be deemed to have taken place. Employees planning to return before the end of the 14 week maternity leave period must give the employer at least seven days' notice. Employers can seek confirmation of the intention to return but the earliest this may be done is 21 days before the end of the maternity leave period.

Q5.6 **What is the difference between Statutory Maternity Pay (SMP) and the Maternity Allowance (MA)?**

A. Statutory Maternity Pay (SMP) is payable to all employees who have 26 weeks of continuous service at the 15th week (the Qualifying Week) before the expected date of childbirth, have stopped working due to the pregnancy, have average earnings above the lower limit for National Insurance Contributions (currently £64 per week), and have given the necessary 21 days' notice of intention to stop work due to pregnancy, as well as providing medical evidence of the expected week of childbirth. Beginning at any time from the 11th week before the expected birth, the SMP lasts for 18 weeks. Current rates are 90% of the average weekly earnings for the first six weeks, and £57.50 for up to 12 weeks thereafter.

Maternity Allowance (MA) is payable by the Benefits Agency to women not eligible for SMP, such as those with less than 26 weeks of continuous service with the current employer or the self-employed. Payable for up to 18 weeks, the employee must have paid National Insurance Contributions (NIC's) for at least 26 weeks in the 66 weeks immediately prior to the expected week of childbirth. MA is not liable to income tax and NIC's, and the employer, having established that the employee is not eligible for SMP, must provide the employee with the maternity certificate and SMP1 within seven days.

Q5.7   What records must I maintain with regards to maternity pay?

A.   Records must be kept for three years after the tax year to which the records refer. You should maintain records as follows:

- the dates of maternity leave and absence
- the weeks for which SMP was paid
- the amount of SMP paid in each week
- the dates and reasons for any non-payments
- the maternity certificates (MATB1) submitted
- copies of any MATB1 forms where the originals have been returned once SMP liability has finished.

As SMP is to be regarded as earnings for social security purposes, the employer must also deduct PAYE and National Insurance Contributions (NIC's), so records must also be kept for the Inland Revenue for claims of reimbursement to be made.

1.   Record SMP payments on the employee's Deduction Working Sheets (P11).

2.   Record the total SMP payments on the employer's End of Year Returns (P14).

3.   Record the total gross SMP payments and the total sum of NIC's on the Annual Statement (P35).

Q5.8   Who pays the Statutory Maternity Pay?

A.   Payments are made by the employer in the same way as any earnings, but the employer can deduct from their next payment of PAYE and National Insurance Contributions (NIC's) to the Inland Revenue a sum equal to 92% of the SMP paid in the preceding tax period. However, 100% of SMP that has been paid out can be deducted for smaller employers if their total NIC liability in the previous tax year was £20,000 or less. They can also get 5.5% of the SMP paid out to cover other associated costs.

Q5.9   What happens if the resumption of work after maternity absence is a problem?

A.   It is unlawful for an employer to dismiss an employee after she resumes work on the grounds that she has taken or availed herself of the benefits of statutory maternity leave. If she has the right to return to work after maternity absence, yet the employer does not permit this to happen, then, subject to the three exceptions noted below, she will be regarded as having been dismissed and may claim unfair dismissal at an Employment Tribunal.

The three exceptions are:

- if the original job is no longer available because of legitimate redundancy and there was no suitable alternative position available
- it was not reasonably practicable (other than redundancy) to take her back in the original position but that a suitable alternative was offered, and the employee either unreasonably refused the offer or accepted it but still claimed dismissal from the original job
- if the employer only employed five or fewer employees, including the employee herself, when her maternity leave period ended

and her additional maternity absence period began, and that it was subsequently impractical to accept the employee back.

All employers should treat these exceptions with great care, especially ensuring that there is no sex discrimination element to their decisions.

6. HEALTH AND SAFETY AT WORK

Q6.1 **As an employer, what are my responsibilities under common law for health and safety matters?**

A. Though much health and safety legislation is now under statute, some key common law and civil liability issues remain, of which employers should be aware. The common law duty requires employers to ensure a safe and healthy place of work, safe plant, appliances and equipment within the workplace, the employment of trained and competent persons, and a safe system of work. All the employer's activities should also be carried out within a duty of care, or civil liability, which ensures that employees are kept safe and healthy in the place of work. If the employer is found to be negligent, then damages may be sought in a civil court, where the employee must prove causal connection between the breach of duty of care and the injuries sustained.

Q6.2 **Who is affected by the Health and Safety at Work Act 1974, particularly over the issue of personal responsibility?**

A. All people at work are covered by the Act, including employers, employees and the self-employed. The only exception is that of domestic servants in a private house. It is also important to note that the legislation is designed to ensure the safety and health of the general public who may be affected by activities in the workplace, notably customers in the hospitality industry. Employers have a responsibility towards every individual (whether employee, contractor or customer) and must have knowledge of particular employees, their abilities, frailties and characteristics (*Paris v Stepney Borough Council* (1951) 1AER 42). Employers also have a duty towards the employees of independent contractors whilst they are on the premises. Furthermore, employees also have a duty to take reasonable care to avoid injury to themselves and others by their work and actions, and must cooperate with the employer over these matters. The general point is that everyone can be held personally responsible for the work that they do, and if found negligent can be prosecuted, and serious offences can lead to fines of up to £20,000 and imprisonment of up to two years.

Q6.3   **What key points should I communicate to employees about the Health and Safety at Work Act 1974?**

A.   In broad terms the Act covers the following three sets of statutory duties.

1.   *The Employers' Duties:* to ensure, so far as is reasonably practicable, the health, safety and welfare at work of all their employees.

2.   *The Employees' Duties:* to take reasonable care for the health and safety at work of themselves and any other people who might be affected by their acts or omissions and to cooperate with their employers and others to enable them to comply with statutory duties and requirements.

3.   *Manufacturers', Designers', Importers', and Suppliers' Duties:* to ensure, as far as is reasonably practicable, that articles are designed and constructed safely, that substances are safe when handled, that necessary tests are carried out and that adequate information is given on the use of articles and substances.

Staff should be aware that the business has a health and safety policy (a requirement for those firms with five or more employees) and be given notice of any changes and additions. In particular, the employer should highlight certain aspects that affect the employee. The element of personal responsibility outlined in Q6.2 is clearly one area to be stressed. Employers must ensure that all employees, whether temporary or permanent (note this also applies to part-time and casual workers) must receive adequate training, instruction and supervision in their work, and be kept fully informed of risks that might affect them and of what to do to reduce those risks. Training in health and safety is recommended by code of practice and is legally required under the **Fire Precautions Act 1971**. It is also important for employers to warn staff that the use of protective clothing and equipment is essential, by pointing out the possible results of not doing so (*Pape v Cumbria County Council* (1992) 3 All ER 211).

Employers should ensure that there is an effective flow of information to all staff, that communication on health and safety matters is fast, and that safety representatives, where they exist, are properly trained and committed to their pivotal role of communicating all relevant matters. It may also be prudent to inform staff that they must not be afraid to use their initiative in potentially dangerous situations. Dismissal is automatically unfair if the actions for which the employee was dismissed were a result of avoiding imminent danger at work, or if he or she was carrying out recognised duties in connection with health and safety.

Q6.4   How is the Health and Safety at Work Act 1974 enforced?

A.   Inspectors may be appointed by the Health and Safety Executive (HSE) or by local authorities; the prime responsibility of these inspectors being to ensure that places of work are complying with all relevant health and safety legislation. Inspectors have right of entry and the power to remove documents, materials and equipment, and to take samples and photographs. They can take immediate action to make safe a dangerous situation, and can carry out full investigations. The inspectors can also issue improvement notices, requiring certain corrective action to be carried out by particular dates, or prohibition notices, banning certain activities and the use of prescribed equipment where they assess that there is a risk of serious personal injury.

Many hotel and catering businesses have developed very good working relationships with local inspectors and environmental health officers (EHO's) by adopting a mature and constructive approach to making improvements. In serious cases of breaches of the legislation or failure to carry out improvement notices, the inspectors do have the power to stop the business trading until the changes have been completed. Appeals against notices can be lodged but the tribunal is likely to be impressed by the expertise of the inspector (*Bellhaven Brewery Co. Ltd v McClean* (1975) IRLR 370). If all notices have failed, then prosecution may result, with fines on conviction of up to £20,000 and imprisonment of up to two years for certain serious offences.

It is also important to note that the concept of corporate offences is now regularly considered by the courts, whereby the negligent actions of one individual, perhaps a supervisor or junior manager, would be considered to have emanated from the direction of more senior management, as embodied by the company (*Tesco Stores Ltd v Nattrass* (1971) 2 All ER 127). In extreme cases, this has been considered as "corporate manslaughter" with directors held personally responsible, as exemplified by the case of the canoeing trip that was so poorly organised that four young people died, and the managing director of the company responsible was found guilty of corporate manslaughter and jailed for three years.

Q6.5   What implications will the Management of Health and Safety Regulations 1992 have on my business?

A.   These regulations came in to effect in January 1993 and were aimed at a general improvement in the management of health and safety issues. Principally, they require employers to adopt a systematic approach to identifying the risks within their workplace and then take whatever action is appropriate to prevent accidents that may result. A summary of the key requirement follows.

1.   Carry out a "risk assessment" to assess all health and safety risks in the workplace, record the findings and take preventive action. The types of risks most likely to be found in the

hospitality industry include lifting, slipping, cutting, burns and the use of dangerous equipment.

2. Appoint sufficient and competent personnel from the workforce to assist, and ensure that they are trained to assess risks and take action. Include the surveillance of health-endangering activities, like noise, fumes and harmful substances.

3. Plan emergency procedures and carry out practice drills, eg fire and bomb threat evacuation procedures.

4. Ensure that all staff, including temporary workers like casuals, or contractors' employees on your premises (eg contract catering staff — see Q6.7) are given full information, training and supervision regarding the specific risks associated with their area of work. Ensure that information is available to all parties concerned, and ensure cooperation and coordination with others such as the contract catering staff employer or others who may be on the premises.

Q6.6   **What health and safety regulations from the 1992 legislation affect me as an employer with regard to the working environment?**

A.   The 1992 health and safety legislation, often referred to as the "six pack", are the main regulations concerned with health and safety in a working environment. There is not the space here to deal with all the details (see section 3 of *Croner's Catering*) but employers should ensure they understand the following points.

1. The **Provision and Use of Work Equipment Regulations 1992** make the employer responsible for the suitability of the equipment in use, its mainenance in good safe working order, the identification of special risks attached to any equipment, and the training, instruction and information of all employees involved in the use, supervision and management of the work processes. Catering enterprises have a great deal of equip-

ment, much of it electrical and potentially dangerous, so check everything in accordance with these regulations, and obtain more information from the Health and Safety Executive (HSE).

2. The **Manual Handling Operations Regulations 1992** require that proper risk assessment is carried out with regard to hazardous manual handling such as the carrying of heavy items over wet or slippery floors. Alternative methods of transporting such goods should be reviewed, including the use of trolleys, and staff should be trained in how to lift properly with less risk of serious back injury, which is a major cause of long-term sickness absence in all industries.

3. The **Workplace (Health, Safety and Welfare) Regulations 1992** cover workplace conditions such as lighting, ventilation and suitability of seating and work areas. There are considerations concerning temperatures in indoor work areas, cleanliness and disposal of waste, the dimensions of work areas and floors, windows and pathways around the work areas as well as basic sanitary and washing facilities. There are also provisions regarding drinking water, lockers, changing rooms, and facilities for rest and eating.

4. The **Personal Protective Equipment at Work Regulations 1992** require employers to review the suitability, provision of protective clothing and apparatus and staff should be given training in their usage. Footwear is of significance for catering operations.

5. The **Health and Safety (Display Screen Equipment) Regulations 1992** require employers to review the suitability of visual display unit (VDU) workers' areas, from safety of the equipment to seating and ventilation. As more and more hospitality work is computerised, for example reservations systems, so these regulations will increase in significance. There is particular reference to planned breaks for staff who

may otherwise spend too many hours looking intently at a VDU screen. Eye tests may need to be provided. As with many of these measures, care and action can lead to much less sickness absence caused by migraine headaches, eye-strain and other related ailments.

Q6.7 **As a contract caterer, how am I affected by the 1992 regulations on health and safety?**

A. Under the **Management of Health and Safety Regulations 1992** a contractor becomes responsible for the safety of his or her staff on another's premises. As a contractor you should be certain that the equipment that your staff will work with is in safe working order. You must ensure that all staff, including casual event staff, for example, are fully trained and instructed in the operation of equipment and other systems in the workplace. This clearly requires a lot of cooperation between the event organiser or contractor and the owner of the premises, so that staff are informed as to the risks prevalent in a particular workplace. Your responsibility also extends to any transport you provide to take contract staff to events and other locations. If you provide the transport, such as a coach, check the safety and maintenance of the vehicle and be sure that the driver is qualified and holds the appropriate licences.

Q6.8 **What exactly is Repetitive Strain Injury (RSI)?**

A. This is the term given to the accepted medical condition whereby the continuous repetition of certain physical tasks can lead to permanent injury and possibly to disability. An alternative expression to describe such conditions is "work-related upper limb disorders", as repetition may only be one of several factors which lead to upper limb musculoskeletal problems. The danger of injury frequently occurs where insufficient and infrequent breaks from a work process are available, or where seating and heights of workstations are inappropriate to the individual. Employers who ignore the complaints and requests from staff, who do not warn staff of the risks, and who do not provide proper breaks and work areas may find themselves paying out large sums in compensation (*McSherry and Lodge v British Telecommunications plc* (1992) 13 Med LR 129). One hospitality example might be the assembly-line type of catering operation for airline meals. In a recent out-of-court settlement, a typist permanently disabled with RSI received £79,000.

Q6.9 **Should I be concerned about legislation on the reporting of dangerous occurrences and the control of dangerous substances?**

A.   Yes. It is a legal requirement under the **Reporting of Injuries, Diseases and Dangerous Occurrences Regulations** (RIDDOR) 1995, that written records of reportable accidents and dangerous occurrences (ie those which must be reported to the appropriate enforcing authority such as the environmental health officer (EHO)) be kept for a minimum of three years. The following must be reported either immediately or within presribed periods and by using form F2508 (revised):

- fatal accidents
- major injury accidents, eg fractures of skull, arm, wrist
- dangerous occurrences, eg wall collapse though no one hurt
- accidents causing more than three days' incapacity for work, including non-working days but excluding the day on which the accident occurred
- certain work-related diseases, eg dysentery or salmonella poisoning in a kitchen
- incidents relating to the gas supply.

More details are available in *Croner's Catering* (section 3) and *Croner's Catering Records and Procedures*.

The **Control of Substances Hazardous to Health Regulations 1988** (COSHH), which came into effect on 1 October 1989 and was updated in 1994, places a duty on employers to reduce employee exposure to dangerous substances. In catering establishments, an assessment should be carried out of the risk of skin contact and absorption, and inhalation, of the many potentially dangerous cleaning materials and chemicals used in hotels and restaurants. Examples could be oven-cleaner, bleach, and drain cleaning fluids. The systematic assessment procedure must be adhered to as outlined in the 1994 amendments, and should include a review of all dust, fumes, vapours and gases generated around the premises. Suppliers of chemicals and cleaning fluids must be contacted to obtain statutory "data-sheets" which give necessary information and warnings about the products. See *Croner's Catering Records and Procedures* and a leaflet entitled *COSHH Assessments* from HMSO.

Q6.10 What level of first aid cover must I ensure, and does it apply to guests as well?

A.   The **Health and Safety First-Aid Regulations 1981** place responsibility upon the employer to ensure that adequate and appropriate equipment and facilities are provided to enable first aid to be rendered to employees if they are injured or become ill at work. This requirement has been strengthened by a code of practice introduced in March 1997 which also stresses the need for each employer to carry out a risk assessment of the business and the jobs therein. There is no obligation under the legislation to take account of non-employees, although this can clearly be done on a voluntary basis. As a guideline, the number of first-aiders needed during normal working hours is one trained and qualified person for every 50 employees. An appointed person, who will take charge of the situation in the absence of a first-aider must be available at all times. It is good practice to attempt to ensure a trained person is always available, especially at night, so perhaps consider training a night porter and/or duty manager for this purpose.

The number of properly stocked first-aid boxes should be sufficient to allow ready access to all employees at work, and details on contents can be obtained from *Croner's Catering* (page 3–106). There is also a code of practice, *First Aid at Work* available from the Stationery Office. There is a legal requirement also to keep a full record of any first-aid treatment administered, as well as a detailed description of any accident in the accident book. See Q6.9 regarding the reporting of serious accidents under the RIDDOR 95 regulations.

Q6.11 **What are the proper procedures when dealing with infectious diseases?**

A. Under the **Food Safety (General Food Hygiene) Regulations 1995**, there is a requirement that any person engaged in the handling of food who becomes aware that he or she is suffering from or is a carrier of any of the conditions noted below, shall immediately inform the employer or representative, who must in turn notify the appropriate medical officer of health for the area. The specific conditions are:

- Typhoid
- Paratyphoid
- Salmonella infections
- Amoebic dysentery
- Bacillary dysentery
- any staphylococcal infection likely to cause food poisoning, eg septic cuts, boils, spots,burns, throat or nasal infections.

Under the **Reporting of Injuries, Diseases and Dangerous Occurrences Regulations 1995** (RIDDOR) employers are required to report cases of specified occupational diseases as they arise, utilising form F2508A, a copy of which should be retained for three years. The full list of diseases and occupations forms part of the relevant regulations and is available from Health and Safety Executive (HSE) area offices. It includes the following.

Checklist: Reportable Health Problems

- poisoning by certain substances, eg arsenic, mercury or phosphorous
- certain skin diseases, eg ulceration, inflammation, or cancer of the skin
- certain respiratory diseases, eg occupational athsma or lung cancer
- certain infections, eg hepatitis, TB or illness caused by a dangerous pathogen
- other conditions, eg bone cancer, cataracts, and white finger.

Q6.12 **What procedures can I introduce to insist that all employees have medical checks and are tested for HIV?**

A. Though reasonable to ask for personal information on health in the form of a confidential, general health questionnaire, and reasonable to insist on a contractually conditional medical examination before the start of employment, there are implications to be aware of which emanate from Article 8 of the European Convention on Human Rights. This dictates that an individual has a right to respect for their private life, and this includes the right to secrecy over a matter of health (*X v Commission of the European Communities* (1995) IRLR 320: ECJ). In this latter case a job applicant refused an HIV test as part of the compulsory medical examination, but secretly, such a test occurred. It is worth noting that the European Court of Justice did express approval of employment-conditional medical examinations, but declared that Article 8 had been breached in this case.

In the absence of an express contractual term, a person with HIV/AIDS is not under an obligation to reveal this unless not to do so would put others at risk of harm or infection, thus breaching s.7 of the **Health and Safety at Work Act**. An employer could make it a condition of employment that a candidate will need to undergo a medical at the employer's expense prior to taking up duties, particularly where aspects of the job make this desirable. In most cases, however, a health questionnaire is considered more than sufficient. This should be part of the recruitment/induction process, and be an element of an overall occupational health policy. Some companies do include on their questionnaire a clause that as a result of the information given, the employer may refer the applicant to a company doctor for examination. Catering firms may introduce also a Food Handlers' Declaration regarding certain infectious diseases (see Q6.11), which, if contracted, must be reported before commencing any food-related work.

General safety advice to employees must stress that the AIDS virus cannot be spread by normal everyday contact, but requires a mix of body fluids. The most sensible precautions for staff are:

- to cover up any cuts or abrasions of their own with waterproof plasters before treating someone else or before being in possible contact with other body fluids

- to avoid contact with blood by wearing gloves

- to use approved chemical cleaning agents to clear up any blood spills.

Larger organisations should devise an AIDS/HIV policy, consulting with staff and obtaining advice from the HSE.

Q6.13 How am I affected by Occupiers Liability?

A.   The increasing availability of leisure facilities in hotels brings with it a need to be aware of the concept of occupier's liability; that the provider of equipment must take reasonable measures to ensure the safety of the premises' equipment. Examples would most commonly be sunbeds, solaria and swimming pools. If you have such facilities you should contact your local environmental health officer (EHO) as different local authorities have brought out a variety of guidance notes and even byelaws concerning these items. These deal with proper installation, the operation by trained individuals, the availability of safety equipment, proper warnings to users of the possible damaging side effects of improper use, and the proper monitoring and analysis of the equipment, including a chemical analysis of swimming pools for quality and sterilent levels. Even if you subcontract your leisure facilities to a specialist firm, you should check on the thoroughness of their procedures for the safety of your customers. Ultimately the occupier of the premises remains liable.

Q6.14 Can an employer be liable for an employee's stress level?

A.   While stress and psychological injury have been serious issues for employers and employees for some time, a recent case has promoted stress at work to a much higher profile. *Walker v Northumberland County Council* (1995) IRLR 35 resulted in a successful claim of unfair dismissal against an employer based on the employer's duty of care. Mr Walker suffered two nervous breakdowns within a year. After returning to work following a period of absence because of the first breakdown, additional assistance was provided but was then withdrawn within a month. The High Court decided that the Council was not responsible for the first illness but was responsible for the second; it was reasonably forseeable that if Mr Walker was again exposed to the same workload and stress then further problems with his health would recur. The Council was in breach of its duty of care, and the Court ruled that an employer has a duty to employees not to cause them psychiatric damage by the volume and character of the work they are required to perform. The Health and Safety Executive (HSE) has issued a guide for employers which outlines the main causes of occupational stress and sets out steps that employers can take to prevent harmful levels of stress in their organisations.

Q6.15 I am considering introducing a policy regarding smoking at work; what should I be aware of?

A.   Whilst smoking by staff in hotel and catering front-of-house areas is clearly controlled by both legal statute and propriety considerations, the issue of smoking in areas such as offices, canteens and other communal sites is worthy of close consideration. As more and more evidence arises concerning the medical dangers of passive smoking, so more cases are coming to court where individuals are claiming that the smoking of work colleagues caused them health problems, and that the management of the business did little or nothing to help the situation. Therefore, under the **Health and Safety at Work Act 1974**, employers have a duty to provide a safe working environment, and this very much includes non-smokers.

A business-wide smoking policy should be formulated following proper consultation with the employees, perhaps certain designated smoking areas could be agreed, or each work area could determine its own policy. However, case law has so far supported employers who, after consultation with staff, have introduced reasonable no-smoking rules (*Dryden v Greater Glasgow Health Board* (1992) IRLR 469), and found against employers who do not respond to the dangers of passive smoking (*Bland v Stockport Borough Council* 1993).

Q6.16 **What are the obligations on me to consult with employees on health and safety matters?**

A.   The **Health and Safety (Consultation with Employees) Regulations 1996** gave non-union members the right to be consulted on health and safety matters in the same way previously afforded to trade union members. The regulations make provision for the appointment of "representatives of employee safety" whose rights in relation to consultation include paid time off to attend appropriate safety committee meetings and access to relevant information. These representatives can, under the law, request that an employer sets up a safety committee as a formal vehicle for discussion and consultation on health and safety issues. A notice must be posted which shows who the members of the committee are, and management representatives must not outnumber employee representatives. Further guidance may be obtained from the Health and Safety Executive (HSE).

Q6.17   What safety measures should I take regarding pregnant employees?

A.   Under the **Employment Rights Act 1996**, where a risk to new or expectant mothers (ie women who are pregnant, have recently given birth or are breastfeeding) has been identified, appropriate preventive safety measures are advised.

1.   Assess whether the work could affect a woman who is pregnant or breastfeeding.

2.   Amend the work if possible to avoid risks occurring.

3.   Make staff aware of the need to reassess any work that could be hazardous to a woman who is pregnant or breastfeeding.

4.   Change working hours or conditions or offer suitable alternative work.

5.   If neither is possible, then it may be necessary to suspend the employee on normal pay for as long as is necessary to protect her health and safety.

Employers are advised to pay particular attention to aspects such as the manual handling of heavy loads, excessive noise, exposure to radiation, chemical agents such as pesticides, and also night work. Under the **Workplace (Health, Safety and Welfare) Regulations 1992**, pregnant and breastfeeding employees must be provided with suitable facilities to rest.

Q6.18   What protection is given to employees regarding their involvement in health and safety matters?

A.   Since 1993, as part of the **Trade Union Reform and Employment Rights Act 1993**, employees have been protected against being dismissed or being put at any other disadvantage for carrying out (or proposing to carry out) certain actions relating to health and safety. The **Employment Rights Act 1996** has consolidated this legislation and it is clearly stated that it is automatically unfair to dismiss employees who:

- are performing health and safety responsibilities designated by their employer

- have left a dangerous part of the workplace if there is believed to be some serious or imminent danger which could not be averted, and are refusing to return whilst the danger persists

- are bringing reasonable health and safety concern to the employer's attention in the absence of a representative or safety committee

- are performing functions as employer-acknowledged health and safety representatives or safety committee members

- are taking appropriate steps to protect themselves or others in circumstances of serious or imminent danger.

Where an employee wishes to bring a claim under these provisions, the matter goes to an Employment Tribunal, and compensation would be awarded if the complaint is well founded.

Q6.19 **Are there any special provisions regarding health and safety and the employment of young people?**

A. Yes, since the **Health and Safety (Young Persons) Regulations 1997** came into effect on 3 March 1997. They include specific risk assessments in the work area, bearing in mind the lack of experience and maturity of these individuals (normally aged between 16 and 18 years). It is also required that information about health and safety arrangements is provided to the young persons and their parents/guardians. Employers should ensure that they have written evidence of the special arrangements and risk assessments undertaken. Young persons must not be given work which is beyond their physical or psychological capacity, nor which involved exposure to toxic substances, and must be fully trained in all aspects of the job to avoid accidents and dangerous occurrencies. However, young persons over 16 years may undertake such work if it is necessary to their training, is fully supervised by a competent person, and where risk is reduced to the lowest level possible. Clearly hospitality employers must take especial care over young apprentices and the like who may be involved in potentially dangerous kitchen, restaurant, or bar work.

7. HARASSMENT

Q7.1 **When does a remark or act by one employee to another become a case of sexual harrassment?**

A. In 1995 the offence of "intentional harassment, alarm or distress" came into effect. This was created by s.4A of the the **Public Order Act 1986**, and makes criminal all forms of harassment (race, sex, sexuality or disability) where it was intentional.

Whilst a dictionary definition of harassment may suggest a continuing or repeated act, a single remark may be of sufficient seriousness to amount to a "detriment" to one sex under s.6(2)(b) of the **Sex Discrimination Act 1975**. At the case of *Institu Cleaning v Heads* (1995) IRLR 4, when a remark was made by a manager to Mrs Heads about her breasts this was clarified. After she had resigned as a result of this incident she claimed unlawful sex discrimination. The employer argued that the remark was not sex-related, as a similiar remark could have been made to a man, for example, about a balding head. The EAT rejected this saying that one remark was sexual the other was not. The EC Recommendation and Code of Practice on sexual harassment refers to "unwanted conduct".

The employer also argued that conduct cannot be "unwanted" until it had occurred and been rejected. The EAT also rejected this claim and said it could be a licence for harassment as a man could always argue that every act of harassment was different from the first and he was testing to see if it was wanted. The code does, therefore, allow for the freedom of choice by the individual to decide what behaviour and from whom he or she finds it acceptable. His or her conduct in relation to persons other than the harasser is irrelevant to a particular case.

Q7.2   How can this be applied at, for example, a Christmas party off the premises?

A.   As stated above it would be a criminal offence, so as far as the two employees are concerned the same criteria would apply. Whether the employer was deemed to be vicariously liable is likely to depend upon whether the event was deemed to be in the "course of employment". It may also depend upon the extent to which the employer prohibited the mode of behaviour during normal working hours. It would also depend on whether it had been an isolated incident or whether there had been other similiar incidents during work.

Q7.3   To what extent is it the employer's responsibility to prevent or control an individual employee's behaviour if it is discriminatory?

A.   There is no express provision in the **Public Order Act 1986** in respect of the employer. However, under s.41 of the **Sex Discrimination Act 1975** and s.32 **Race Relations Act 1976** employers are vicariously liable for the discriminatory actions of their employees if those actions occur in the course of employment, even if the employer has no knowledge of, or has not sanctioned, those actions. Employers may be able to show that they are not liable if reasonably practical steps have been taken to prevent discriminatory acts by employees. It is therefore in an employer's interest to take preventive measures, such as having a clear policy against harassment and making it clear to employees that it is a serious disciplinary offence.

Q7.4   How should a complaint from an employee that a colleague is "calling them names" be dealt with?

A.   The normal procedure for a grievance should be followed. Whether on the grounds of sex or race, the question of detriment (see Q1.14 and Q1.17) must be borne in mind, ie neither one must be treated less favourably than the other. It must be considered that a full, fair investigation is carried out which may result in adequate steps being taken to ensure the two employees continue their employment satisfactorily. This may involve the transfer of one of the employees to another department, where possible.

Q7.5 **If two employees are known to be involved in a personal relationship, what rights does an employer have concerning this situation?**

A. In essence the individuals concerned are two employees, and their behaviour at the workplace should not be treated any differently to other employees. Some organisations have a policy on employees and personal relationships. If this is the case then it must be made clear at the commencement of employment exactly what that policy is, the action those concerned must take and the likely outcome in terms of action, if any, by the employer (*Coleman v Skyrail Oceanic Ltd* 1981 IRLR 398).

8. RECORDS, REFERENCES AND DATA PROTECTION

Q8.1 **What records am I obliged to keep by law regarding my employees?**

A. There are some records that you are obliged to keep by law. These are:

– Pay As You Earn (PAYE) and National Insurance records

– Statutory Maternity Pay (SMP) and Statutory Sick Pay (SSP) records

– Reporting of Injuries, Diseases and Dangerous Occurrences Regulations (RIDDOR) records (see Q6.9)

– Working Time Regulations (see Q8.5).

Other than these, in case of any unfair dismissal claims or similar actions, you are advised to keep:

– a copy of any contract of employment

– a copy of any written statement of terms and conditions given to employees, as required by the **Employment Rights Act 1996,** and all amendments to these

– copies of any disciplinary warnings, etc issued to individual employees.

Q8.2 **What records must I keep for the selection of a candidate?**

A. There are no legal requirements to keep any specific records. However it is good practice, and advisable, to keep records of the following:

– personnel specification and job description

– total number of applicants

– those interviewed

– standard questions asked

- objective criteria for those turned down (preferably a standard format of assessment as provided in *Croner's Catering Records & Procedures*)

This will provide what would be necessary should a claim of discrimination be made against a prospective employer.

Q8.3   What rights do employees have to see the information kept about them?

A.   Any data recorded on a computer has been subject to the **Data Protection Act 1984** which sets out to protect information held about people. In order to meet the requirements of the **EC Data Protection Directive 1995**, this has been updated by the **Data Protection Act 1998** which gives employees rights of access to virtually all personal files kept on them by their employers — this includes manual records.

The **Data Protection Act 1998** extends the 1984 Act as follows:

- includes manual records held within a "relevant filing system"
- broadens the definition of date to include "obtaining, recording or holding the data... adaptation or alteration... or use of data"
- access must be given to the employee although notice may be requested in writing and a fee may be charged for any permanent copies issued
- employees will not have the right to access references or succession planning information
- covers all files that identify the employee
- there are likely to be tighter controls on *sensitive* data eg race, religious beliefs, sexual orientation, health, TU membership and political views.

It also states appropriate measures to prevent unauthorised processing must be in place.

For further details contact the CBI, tel: 0171-379 7400 or a legal advisor.

Q8.4   To what extent can information concerning salaries be "open" within the company?

A.   Under the **Data Protection Act 1998**, payroll data must not be disclosed except in the following circumstances:

- to any person responsible for making the payments
- for the purpose of obtaining actuarial advice
- for research into occupational diseases
- where the individual concerned has consented to the disclosure (eg for mortgage applications)
- for audit purposes
- to provide information about the person's financial affairs (eg in the event of a policy inquiry)

If you have a clear job evaluation scheme you may be able to publicise job gradings for recruitment or promotion purposes.

Q8.5   What records do the Working Time Regulations require?

A.   The Regulations key points include the following:

1.   *A maximum working week.* Employees must not work more than 48 hours per week over any 17 week period (this is a rolling period of time). This 48 hour limit includes overtime worked.

2.   *Entitlement to rest breaks.*

  (a)   *per day:* a break of at least 20 minutes after 6 consecutive hours of work should be provided to all employees. An adult worker is entitled to not less than 11 consecutive hours of rest in each 24 hour period (see shift workers below)

  (b)   *per week:* an adult worker is entitled to an uninterrupted period of rest of not less than 24 hours in each 7 day period. Over a 14 day period the rest period may be back-to-back (ie one 48 hour rest period)

(c)   *shift workers:* adult workers changing shift from one time to another are exempt from the daily and weekly rest requriement, similarly those working on a split shift

The regulations do say that those employees who have surges of activity (eg tourism) and those who travel between different places of work for one employer may be exempt from the rest breaks and night-time working rules. However, where possible compensatory rest times should be made available.

3.   *Annual leave.* For the first time in the UK there is now legislation for employers to provide at least 3 weeks paid leave per annum (beginning on or before 23 November 1998). After 23 November 1999 this will increase to 4 weeks entitlement. Leave days cannot be carried over to the next holiday year, and when an employee leaves the employer is obliged to pay for any untaken leave that is due. (An employer can similarly deduct payment from the last pay for any leave over and above what is due at the time of termination.

4.   *Night workers.* Those working between 2300hrs and 0600hrs (although an agreement may be made with the employee to set a different period which must include midnight to 0500hrs)

(a)   a night worker's hours are not to exceed 8 hours for each period of 24 (over a 17 week period)

(b)   night workers whose jobs involve "heavy physical or mental strain" should never work more than 8 hours in each 24 hour period

(c)   they also have right to free health checks at regular intervals. Any daytime worker can be assigned night time work but must be provided with a free health assessment.

5.   *Exemptions to the Regulations* include "mobile" workers involved in transport (air, rail, road, sea, inland waterway and lake), but this does not include catering or cleaning staff at airports, seaports, etc who are covered by the Regulations.

People whose working time "is not measured or pre-determined or can be determined by the worker himself" — this seems to include managerial executives or others with autonomous decision-making powers, family workers and church officials, but it is not clear whether it would include, for example, sales executives and all managers or only senior executives.

6.   *Opt-out.* The regulations make provision for individuals to agree voluntarily to work more than 48 hours per week. If this is the case it *must be in writing*, and may include a time period (including indefinitely) and the employee has the right to terminate this agreement at any time by giving the employer not less than 7 days' notice in writing. Collective and workforce agreements cannot alter the 48 hour rule. (See also Q1.28.)7.

7.   *Record-keeping.* The **Working Time Regulations 1998** require employers to maintain up to date records of all employees' times worked and their written agreements where applicable. These records must be kept for up to two years and an HSE inspector may inspect them at any time and restrict or prohibit any extensions agreed.

Full details are available from HMSO No. 1833.

A booklet is available from the Labour Research Department 78, Blackfriars Road, London SE1 8HF. Tel: 0171-928 3649.

Records of rotas, shifts worked (including overtime records) are therefore necessary to be able to assess an on-going situation.

Q8.6   Am I obliged to give a reference concerning an ex-employee or one about to leave my employment?

A.   You are not obliged by law to give a reference concerning an employee or ex-employee, though obviously the vast majority of employers do give references. Assessing a new employee's competence for a job would be made much more difficult without this practice.

Q8.7 **Can an ex-employee bring an action against me as a result of a reference I have written?**

A. When an employer gives a reference he or she should tell the truth. Truthful references will create few problems for the employer writing them, although in theory an employee could sue for defamation if a reference contained an unprovable statement. References are covered by "qualified privilege" which means that an employer can be sued only if he or she acted "maliciously". It is very difficult to prove malice in a court of law and as there is no legal aid for defamation cases it is very unlikely that an employee will bring an action for defamation. Many employers limit such a risk by only giving oral references by telephone.

Q8.8 **Can employees see references I have received about them or can past employees ask for details of references I have written about them?**

A. It would appear that if the reference is kept on a computer then the employee will have a right of access to it under the **Data Protection Act 1998**. Should a dispute go to court then a reference may have to be produced to the court.

Q8.9 **Am I responsible to another employer as a result of a reference I provide for him or her concerning an ex-employee of mine?**

A. If in providing a reference to another employer you knowingly give false or misleading information, you may be liable for negligence. However, no such cases have been recorded recently. You may limit your liability by writing "without prejudice" across the top of a reference.

If employers deliberately provide false references or an employee forges or alters a reference they can be prosecuted in a magistrates' court under the **Servants' Character Act 1792**.

9. RELATIONSHIPS WITH TRADE UNIONS

Q9.1   Is an employer obliged to recognise and negotiate with a trade union which claims to have a significant number of his or her employees as members?

A.   As at September 1998 recognition of a trade union is entirely within the control of the employer. This may well change shortly. The employer can choose to recognise or not recognise a trade union. "Recognition" normally means that an employer is willing to negotiate with a union on some or all of the following matters:

– terms and conditions of employment and/or physical working conditions

– employments termination or suspension of employment or duties of one or more workers

– allocation of work between workers

– disciplinary matters

– membership or non-membership of a union by a worker

– facilities for union officials

– negotiation or consultation machinely.

Whether or not to recognise a union can be important because it is only recognised unions who have the right to have certain information disclosed to them.

Q9.2   Can I refuse to employ someone because of their membership of a trade union?

A.   No. Section 137 of the **Trade Union and Labour Relations Act 1992** makes it unlawful to refuse employment to someone on grounds of their union membership.

Q9.3   **Can I refuse to employ someone because of their refusal to join a trade union?**

A.   Again the answer is no. As written in the preceding answer, s.137 of the **Trade Union and Labour Relations Act 1992** makes it unlawful to refuse employment to someone on grounds of their union membership, ie because a person is or is not a member of a trade union or because he or she is unwilling to accept such a requirement.

Q9.4   **Am I obliged to have a means of consulting with staff on any matters concerning their employment?**

A.   In principle, (as at September 1998) there are few regulations in the UK (when compared to Continental Europe) concerning the creation or operation of consultative arrangements between management and staff. This is likely to change as more European law is adopted. Currently the important exceptions are concerned with redundancy and safety.

1.   **Redundancy.** An employer who recognises an independent trade union in respect of a group of employees must consult with the trade union if he or she plans to make any members of that union redundant. The following time limits apply:

  • 10–99 employees: at least 30 days before the first dismissals take effect

  • 100 or more employees: at least 90 days before the first dismissals take effect

  (Trade Union and Labour Relations (Consolidation) Act 1992 s.193, as amended).

2.   **Health and safety.** In the case of health and safety matters the **Safety Representatives and Safety Committees Regulations 1977** require an employer to form a safety committee when so requested by two or more employees.

3. The **Transfer of Undertakings (Protection of Employment) Regulations** (SI 1794) requires that before a transfer takes place an employer must consult with any employee representatives. These may be union representatives or employee representatives elected by the employees.

Q9.5 **What information do employers have to give their employees about matters concerning their employment?**

A. The Advisory, Conciliation and Arbititration Service (ACAS) has issued a Code of Practice on Disclosure of Information. The Code suggests that the following subjects should be included:

- pay and benefits
- conditions of service
- employment, eg numbers employed, categories of employee
- productivity and any savings, improvements
- financial matters.

All employers who employ on average more than 250 people, whether they recognise a union or not, are obliged to include in the annual directors' report information on the following:

- matters of concern to the employees
- consultation arrangements encouraging employee involvement
- financial and economic factors affecting employee performance.

Q9.6 **What information has to be given to a recognised trade union?**

A. The **Trade Union and Labour Relations (Consolidation) Act 1992** imposes a duty on employers who recognise trade unions for the purpose of collective bargaining to provide union representatives (when requested in writing) with information which is:

(a) information without which the representatives would be impeded in carrying on collective bargaining to a material extent, and

(b)   information which should be disclosed to them for the purpose of collective bargaining in accordance with good industrial relations practice.

Employers are not obliged to disclose the following information:

(a)   information against the national interest

(b)   information the disclosure of which would result in contravention of a prohibition or an enactment

(c)   information acquired in confidence

(d)   information about an individual unless he agrees to the disclosure

(e)   information likely to damage the employer's business for reasons other than its effect on collective bargaining

(f)   information obtained by the employer which is concerned with legal proceedings.

In addition a union has the right to be consulted on a number of issues including:

– health and safety (**Health and Safety at Work Act, 1974**)

– occupational pensions (**Social Security Act 1975**)

– redundancy*

– transfer of undertakings*.

*Collective Redundancies and Transfer of Undertakings (Protection of Employment (Amendment) Regulations 1995 (SI 1995 No. 2587).

Q9.7   What rights to time off do union members have?

A.   Union officials have the right to time off from work, with pay, to carry out trade union duties and undergo industrial relations training.

Other union members may be allowed to take part in union activities without pay. (Section 137 of the **Trade Union and Labour Relations Act 1992**).

Q9.8 **Can I dismiss someone because they took part in trade union activities at a time inconvenient to the business?**

A. Employees who take time off without permission are in breach of their employment contract and can be subject to appropriate disciplinary action. However, employees who are also union officials and who are members of a recognised union are allowed to take reasonable time off during working hours to take part in activities of that union or where the employee is representing that union. This should, however, be with the agreement of the employer.

Any industrial action is excluded from this legislation so employees taking time off, for example to strike, are technically in breach of contract and could be subject to discipline including possibly dismissal.

Q9.9 **Can I dismiss someone because they took part in industrial activities, eg a strike?**

A. As written above, employees who take time off without permission are in breach of their employment contract and can be subject to appropriate disciplinary action. So employees taking time off to strike are technically in breach of contract and could be subject to discipline, including possibly dismissal.

However, all employees involved in the action must be treated in a similar way — otherwise there may be grounds for an action for unfair dismissal. (Sections 237 and 238 of the **Trade Union and Labour Relations Act 1992**.)

Q9.10 **Can a trade union be sued for damages arising from inducing breaches of contracts of employment?**

A. Trade unions used to benefit from certain "immunities" in law. This gave them a privileged position in that they could not be sued for their liabilities arising from industrial action. Union disputes only benefit from immunity in civil law if the dispute is between the employer and his or her employees and if a proper ballot of the members has been conducted.

Secondary action, such as picketing a supplier's premises, is therefore not subject to any immunity and those concerned can be sued for damages. If unlawful action is authorised by a union, an injured party may sue the union for damages (**Trade Union and Labour Relations Act 1992**).

The main exception to this rule on secondary picketing is that the employees concerned are allowed to persuade other workers, such as delivery drivers, not to cross a picket line at the place of employment of the striking workers.

Q9.11   Does the "closed" shop still exist?

A.   A "closed shop" traditionally referred to a place of work where the employer had an agreement with a union that all employees (or certain categories) would be or would become members of the union. The **Trade Union and Labour Relations Act 1992** has made the "closed shop" inoperative, mainly because employers can no longer oblige workers to join a union.

Q9.12   As an employer am I obliged to help a union to conduct a ballot on our premises?

A.   Under Trade Union Ballot Regulations an employer is obliged, so far as is reasonable, to allow his or her premises to be used for a union ballot by employees who are union members. This only applies where the employer and any associated employer employ more than 20 employees the trade union is recognised by the union for collective bargaining. If an employer refuses, the union can present a complaint to a trade union.

Q9.13   Is an employer obliged to operate a "check-off" system, ie collect union subscriptions on the union's behalf?

A.   There is no legal requirement for employers to make deductions on the union's behalf. However, many employers agree to do so in the interests of good relationships with their employees and the union concerned.

If an employer agrees to operate a "check-off" system there are certain conditions in order for the deduction to be legal:

- that the employee has authorised the deduction in writing within the last three years and has not subsequently withdrawn it (s.13 **Employment Rights Act 1996**)

- that the employer has notified the employee of any increase in subcription and has reminded the employee that he or she can withdraw the authorisation at any time.

10. TRANSFER OF UNDERTAKINGS

Q10.1 **If I am not a catering contractor, presumably these regulations do not apply to me. Is that correct?**

A.   The **Transfer of Undertakings (Protection of Employment) Regulations 1981 SI 1794** was designed to implement the EC Directive on Acquired Rights (77/187/EEC).

In the catering industry they had their greatest significance at the time of Compulsory Competitive Tendering (CCT) of public sector services. Public sector organisations were very concerned that contractors would undercut them in the bidding process, particularly on staffing costs, as they felt that the private sector did not offer such good terms and conditions of employment. The regulations essentially were there to protect employees' continued service and terms and conditions of employment after a transfer.

The regulations apply to transfers of businesses which are effected by sale or other disposition or by operation by law. They cover the transfer of commercial undertakings from one person to another as long as it is the business itself which is being disposed of. Relevant transfers would include the sale of a business to a new owner, the merger of two companies, or the integration of a subsidiary's activities within a parent company's business, "providing that both the assets and the business are transferred".

However, it could equally potentially apply in a situation in which cleaning services in a hotel were given to a commercial contractor. This area has provided considerable work for the tribunals in recent years, and there have been some changes in interpretation of the law in the light of recent European rulings, some of which have offered very different interpretation of the law. These rulings have focused particularly on the phrases "commercial undertakings" and also "providing that both the assets and the business are transferred". These two points will be further developed in the questions below.

The aim of the Regulations is to protect the employment of employees who are affected by the transfer. Regulation 8 (1) states that a dismissal will be regarded as unfair where an employee is dismissed because of the transfer, or for a reason connected with it.

Q10.2 **If a ruling is made that there is a transfer of business and TUPE does apply, do I have to take on board all the staff's accrued benefits, etc?**

A.   Generally, yes. Employees receive continuity of employment. The only possible area of incompatibility being related to occupational pension schemes, where it is doubtful that schemes would be identical. However, it is currently being debated if the new employer should offer pension schemes which are no less favourable to the employee. Clearly this would have major significance to employers. This emphasises the need to establish details in any tendering process of what the precise liability towards employees could be.

Q10.3 **Will TUPE apply in every situation regarding the "takeover" of a service?**

A.   In 1994 there was a far reaching decision by the European Court of Justice concerning the interpretation of the EC acquired rights directive and impact on the TUPE regulations. It was that of *Schmidt v Spar-und Leihkasse der fruheren Amter Bordesholm, Kiel und Cronshagen* (1994 IRLR 302). It concerned a lady who was employed by the bank as a cleaner. She was then dismissed when the cleaning was contracted out. In this case it was decided that the decisive factor in determining if a transfer has taken place is whether the business retains its identity; in other words, is the new employer resuming or continuing the same or similar activities? This interpretation did not have regard for the transfer of the assets of the business as stated in our TUPE regulations. This meant that virtually all contracting-out operations would be considered as transfers of business. Subsequent to the *Schmidt* ruling, the Court of Appeal followed the ruling over the transfer of a contracted cleaning service in the health sector (*Dines v (1) Initial Health Care Services Ltd (2) Pall Mall Services Group Ltd* (1994 IRLR 336).

However, more recently there have been some rulings which have reached different conclusions, but using a variety of different criteria for their judgment. One decision by the EAT concerned the transfer of a catering business from Compass UK to Brian Smith Catering which the EAT decided was not a transfer as no goodwill was transferred and there was nothing in the nature of a business to transfer.

More recently, another case in Germany, that of *Ayse Suzen v Zehnacker Gebaudereinigung GmbH Krankenhausservice and Lefarth GmbH* (1997 IRLR 255) offered a different view. In this case a woman again was employed as a cleaner, and was dismissed following the loss by her employer of a cleaning contract. The ruling stated that she could not automatically claim to be an employee of the incoming company who had won the cleaning contract. The court ruled that simply because the service carried out by the new company was similar did not automatically mean a transfer of economic entity.

They ruled that in the absence of a transfer of assets or taking over of an "essential" part of the workforce, the directive is not applicable. Thus, there is now some doubt about the "essential" workforce, and whether this means a majority of the workforce, and whether this is in to whether "assets" include intangibles such as "expertise". The result of this, of course, is that there is now considerable confusion on this issue, and the transfer can no longer be seen as being automatic, as was the case after the *Schmidt* ruling. Legal advice must be sought on each individual case to establish the position. The European Commission is to consider amendments to the Acquired Rights

Directive, which could include the old and new "owner" of an undertaking having joint and several responsibility to employees, and also the requirement for the new owner to offer pension rights which are at least as good as those provided by the previous owner.

Q10.4 **If a catering or other contract changed hands, do the staff all have to be made redundant or could some be transferred?**

A.   This is now unclear as a result of the conflicting judgments of the *Schmidt* and *Ayse Suzen* cases. It is suggested that legal advice be taken until further clarification from the European Commission is received. In cases where staff have transferred in the past, it has not always been the case that employees are replaced when they subsequently leave their job. Hence, potential savings in the operation of contracts could be made by not replacing "natural wastage", thus saving on personnel costs. In addition, in the normal running of operations, an organisation does have the right to change its terms and conditions of employment, provided that it gives its employees appropriate notice of this.

Q10.5 **At the time of a transfer of business, can an incoming contractor offer terms and conditions of service that are less favourable to the employees?**

A.   No, as this would not constitute a precise continuation of the employment contract.

Q10.6 **If not all relevant information was disclosed to me when I took over a contract, what action can I take?**

A.   The only action is to sue through the courts. This will usually take the form of an incoming business or contractor suing the outgoing operator for giving inaccurate information (misrepresentation) about its current employees terms and conditions, which results in miscalculations on their tender bid.

Q10.7 **If an employee is dismissed as a result of a "transfer", can that employee claim compensation for unfair dismissal?**

A.   Yes, if the dismissal is as a result of the transfer, either before or after it takes place. To claim unfair dismissal the employees must have been employed for 104 weeks continuously (reducing to 52 weeks in the latter part of 1999). Dismissals around the time of the transfer are likely to be regarded by a tribunal as being for a transfer-related reason.

Q10.8 **By law, what information of my employees' pay and benefits do I have to provide to a prospective future provider of current services?**

A.   There is no legal guidance available, however the following should be regarded as the minimum:

– names, job titles, start date, and current salary of all employees

– normal hours for all employees

– holiday and sickness entitlement for all employees — information on membership of pension schemes

– details of benefits-in-kind.

11. REDUNDANCIES

Q11.1 **What is redundancy — is it just losing one's job?**

A.   Redundancy has a specific meaning in employment law and will occur in one of the following circumstances:

- an entire business or particular work location closes down
- a job disappears
- there is a reduction in an employer's need for employees to carry out a particular type of work — this might be as a result in the amount of work to be done, or a change in working practice.

Redundancy therefore is about a job and not really the individual person doing it.

Q11.2 **If I give a former employee a letter to say that they were made redundant as a reason for dismissal, will that help prevent claims to tribunals?**

A.   No, because an employer has specific responsibilities in a redundancy situation regarding, for example, period of notice to be given, basis of selection of staff for redundancy, and the need to consult with employee representatives. Hence, this too could lead to potential problems. In all dismissal cases it is essential that you give the exact reason for dismissal and are able to substantiate facts relating to the dismissal.

Q11.3 **What general guidance is there on the selection of employees for redundancy?**

A.   Redundancy selection procedures may be covered in a procedural agreement with workers representatives, or an organisation may have a customary arrangement. However, an employer's selection criteria should be objective and should be capable of being verified by reference to data.

An employer will have to prove that criteria are fair and have been objectively and equally applied to all employees concerned.

In the past, the concept of "last in first out" (LIFO) has been applied by many, but there have been challenges that this is indirectly discriminatory against women, who tend to have more job breaks than men.

ACAS has a code of practice for dealing with redundancy, and this should be reflected in individual organisations' methods. If redundancies are to be expected then it is advisable to plan for this by allowing natural wastage and the recruitment of temporary employees so as to reduce the number of enforced redundancies. Safer criteria include opting for those over normal retirement age first, followed by those who wish to volunteer.

Employers will not like to lose enthusiastic, skilled employees and so objective selection based on skills and qualifications will be more suited to the needs of the business.

Criteria which is often used in redundancy selection includes:

– attendance

– age and fitness

– ability skills and experience

– performance, and

– length of service.

Negatives such as a poor disciplinary record and absenteeism may also be used, but it is vital that decisions are based on facts and the criteria is used to judge all staff concerned, in order to be consistent. An employer will therefore have to show that there has been a comparative analysis of appropriate data relating to all pertinent employees.

All this indicates the need to have sound procedures in place, and good records relating to discipline, absenteeism, and work performance.

Dismissal for redundancy will be automatically unfair if the employee was selected for a reason relating to trade union membership or in contravention of an agreed procedure or customary arrangement. Redundancy due to pregnancy would also be automatically unfair.

Q11.4   Do I have to pay redundancy pay in all circumstances?

A.   There are statutory minimum payments, but an employer may also have an agreement with its employees to enhance these payments. Statutory payments are based on age and length of continuous service, and are as follows:

- 1 week's pay for each year of employment between the ages of 22–41

- 1.5 week's pay for the each year of employment over the age of 41

- 0.5 a week's pay for each year of employment under the age of 21.

Employees who have reached their normal retiring age are not entitled to a statutory redundancy payment, even if that age is less than 65. That age must be the same for male and female employees doing the same job. If it is not possible to establish a "normal" retiring age, that will be 65.

Q11.5   If staff are absent on maternity leave when redundancies are made, should they receive redundancy pay?

A.   If their previous job ceases to exist then they have the same rights to compensation as anyone else. It is important, therefore, that you include such staff. If a female employee has had a break for maternity but has now returned to your employment, you should count the time when she was away on approved maternity leave, as this counts as continuous service. The Statement of Terms and Conditions of Employment is a very important document in this situation, and should indicate the date on which continuous service commenced. Currently, all staff with a minimum two years continuous service will qualify for State redundancy pay.

Q11.6 What are my obligations regarding consultation with the workforce?

A. In most cases an employer who fails to consult with employees is going to be guilty of unfairly dismissing them. This became clear from the House of Lords in *Polkey v A E Dayton Services Ltd* (1987 IRLB 503):

> In the case of redundancy, the employer will normally not act reasonably unless he warns and consults any employees affected or their representatives, adopts a fair basis on which to select for redundancy and takes such steps as may be reasonable to avoid or minimise redundancy by re-deployment within his own organisation.

Notice of dismissal should not be issued until consultation has taken place. Initially, plans to avoid redundancies should be considered.

The consultation should include the following:

- an explanation of the need for redundancies
- an explanation of why particular employees have been identified as candidates for redundancy
- an explanation of marking under any selection criteria
- an explanation of why the employer has not been able to offer alternative work
- the employees should be allowed to make comments on any of the points.

If an organisation recognises a trade union or if there is any other body that represents their interests, such as a staff association for the category of employees who are being dismissed, there are some statutory time limits set out regarding consultation:

(a) where the employer is proposing to dismiss as redundant 100 or more employees at one establishment within a period of

90 days or less, at least 90 days notice before the first of those dismissals takes effect, or

(b) where the employer is proposing to dismiss as redundant 10 or more employees at one establishment within a period of 30 days or less, at least 30 days notice before the first of those dismissals takes effect.

Q11.7 Do I have to offer alternative employment to a redundant employee if it is available?

A. You do have to offer suitable alternative employment if it is available. Employers have an obligation to see what alternative vacancies exist not only in their own company, but also in associated companies. Also it should not be assumed that an employee is not prepared to work for less money, or on shorter hours. It is good practice to circulate vacancies to redundant employees and then invite applicants. If employers do not look for alternative employment or make assumptions about what jobs employees may accept, and therefore not offer them, there could be a justifiable case for unfair dismissal (*Nationwide Anglia Building Society v Hooper* (EAT 360/91)).

Q11.8 Can an employee refuse to accept alternative employment, and would this affect their rights to a redundancy payment?

A. They can reject alternative employment if they feel that the alternative employment is unreasonable. The **Employment Rights Act 1996** provides that "if the employee unreasonably refuses a suitable offer of employment, he is not entitled to a redundancy payment". The question of reasonableness is one that often could only be decided by a tribunal.

Q11.9 I have a mobility clause in my statement of terms and conditions of employment, and have vacancies in a nearby operation. The staff, however, claim that they are entitled to a

redundancy payment. Can I not make them redundant, transfer them, and hence not make a redundancy payment?

A. In the case of *High Table Ltd v Horst* (Court of Appeal), three waitresses at one location were dismissed as redundant and claimed unfair dismissal on the basis that there were jobs available in other locations. The case rested on the definition of "the place where the employee was so employed". The Court of Appeal took the view that all three had worked at one location for some considerable time, and a reduction in work at that location was sufficient to satisfy the statutory definition of redundancy. Thus, the term in the contract on mobility was not enforceable in this situation. It would appear that if mobility clauses are to be enforced, then staff should be moved from one location to another to illustrate that this indeed is a "current and live" term of employment.

Q11.10 Do I have to look for alternative employment for staff who are currently on maternity leave?

A. Yes. Staff on maternity leave are regarded as employees if they have stated their right to return to work after the appropriate period of time. They should not be forgotten when looking for suitable alternative employment.

Q11.11 What is the basis of the calculation of an average weekly wage?

A. An average weekly wage is comprised of two factors: the normal working hours and the average hourly rate. Normal hours are those stipulated in the Conditions of Employment. This would not normally include overtime unless it is a requirement of the employer that this overtime is always worked, and hence a condition of employment. Overtime hours can not be counted unless a fixed amount has been agreed *which was obligatory on both sides*. There have been a number of cases on this issue, where tribunals have allowed overtime to be calculated as part of the normal hours, but these have often been overturned by the EAT or the Court of Appeal (*Tarmac Roadstone Holdings v Peacock* 1973 ICR 273).

Where there is no normal working week, this is calculated as the average number of hours over the 12 weeks prior to the calculation date. (See *Croner's Employment Law,* G63–67).

The maximum amount that can be calculated for a week's pay for redundancy purposes, and also payments for unfair dismissal, is set by the Secretary of State for Employment.

Q11.12 What is a claim for unfair selection for redundancy?

A.   This is essentially a claim for unfair dismissal in which the former employee is contesting the basis of their selection for redundancy. This will usually occur if it is in breach of an agreement between an employer and his or her employees concerning redundancy selection.

Q11.13 Do I have to give time off and training to employees who may be made redundant?

A.   Yes. Employees who have been given notice of dismissal by reason of redundancy, are entitled to "reasonable time off during working hours for the purpose of looking for new employment or to make arrangements for training". Many employers set up job hunting facilities on their premises if they have to make a large number of redundancies. Increasingly organisations are employing specialist consultants to help employees present themselves at job interviews, and to design attractive CVs. This is in addition to counselling for those staff requiring it.

Q11.14 For how long can employees "try out" a new job without losing their rights to redundancy pay?

A.   Employees are allowed a trial period of up to four weeks to enable them to assess if alternative employment is suitable and acceptable to them. The legislation states that "an employee who unreasonably terminates or gives notice to terminate a new contract of suitable employment during the trial period loses the right to a payment".

12. DISCIPLINARY ACTION

Q12.1   Should all disciplinary action take the same form?

A.   Any organisation's disciplinary procedure should be laid out in the Statement of Terms and Conditions of Employment. This is important, as if problems with employees lead to tribunal hearings, then the tribunal will be keen to establish that a procedure was in place, and that it was followed correctly. Such procedures should follow the ACAS Code of Disciplinary Practice and Procedure. This process will involve oral and written warnings in most cases, which could lead to a final warning and perhaps dismissal.

What will vary will be the response you will expect to get from an employee. For a matter of misconduct, you can expect an immediate response, whereas for unsatisfactory performance it may take a little time to reach the required standards.

Q12.2   If employees are not performing satisfactorily, should I immediately commence disciplinary action?

A.   A disciplinary procedure is not simply a series of stages leading to a dismissal. Its aims are also to encourage employees to improve their performance or to stop breaking rules. It can be likened to a referee in a soccer match who may well talk to players before issuing a "yellow card" (warning). However, if an employee's performance is not up to standard (potential incapability), the employer should take steps to improve it, for example by giving further training or instruction, if appropriate.

It is good practice to record such training in the event of there being a need for formal disciplinary procedures at a later date.

In this instance, it is also important to give an employee ample time to improve, and not expect an "instant cure". Performance should then be reviewed at an agreed date in the future.

Q12.3   What must I do to ensure that employees are aware of company rules, etc?

A.   Knowledge of company rules is vital for all employees, but especially new staff, who will be unaware of what general rules apply within an organisation. A breach of house rules could lead to "employee misconduct", and clearly a new employee could break a rule within a few hours or days of starting a job. This is especially true in the catering industry where employers have different rules about, for example, eating and drinking on duty. The problem of employees taking home waste food, is another potential problem for the employer. All rules must be stated clearly, and applied consistently. The time of the employees induction is an obvious time for this. Those that operate some form of employee induction record card, perhaps with an employee signature indicating that they have had rules explained to them, will act as a useful record (see *Croner's Catering Records and Procedures*). The induction period should also be used to explain the organisation's disciplinary procedures. In addition to explaining rules, it is also important that an employee can see them being employed consistently to all employees by the employer or supervisor. This consistency applies not only to rule adherence and tolerance but also in the application of laid down procedures.

It should be noted that a failure to follow the laid down procedure could lead to a dismissal being found to be unfair, in spite of what may appear to be valid grounds for disciplinary action.

Q12.4   If malpractice by employees has been taking place for some time, am I allowed to dismiss them for it?

A.   You are, but you may not be able to do it as quickly as you would like. If you have been turning a blind eye to some malpractice, even though it is listed in disciplinary rules, then it may be difficult to defend dismissal for this. What you must do is to restate the rules through the disciplinary procedures, and perhaps via a staff meeting, and then be consistent in enforcing the rule with all employees. When it has been re-established that such behaviour is not acceptable, disciplinary action may be needed if malpractice continues. It should be remembered, however, that you should follow your disciplinary procedure as suggested by the ACAS Code of Practice.

Q12.5 Can I withhold pay for employees found guilty of misconduct?

A. No. Employees have carried out their part of a contract of employment by supplying their labour, and therefore should be paid for it. The house rules, however, may allow for employees to be dismissed without receiving paid notice or receiving accrued holiday pay in cases of gross misconduct. Employees should, of course, be made aware of this.

Q12.6 Do employees have a right of representation during disciplinary procedures?

A. Yes. The ACAS Code of Practice on disciplinary procedures suggests that employees have a right of representation, and this should be written into your disciplinary procedures, which include a right of appeal. The representation can be by an employee representative, or simply a "friend". It is also good practice for the employer also to have a witness present at such interviews. In addition, thorough records of any such meetings should be made by the employer.

Q12.7 In what circumstances might it be appropriate to suspend an employee?

A. Where it is not possible to investigate a case fully at the time. This allows pressure of the heat of the moment to pass, so that there is a better chance of a cool, rational decision being taken. It also allows time to talk to other personnel who may be able to contribute to the investigation. Sometimes those with the authority to conduct disciplinary interviews may not be present at all times, so suspension, again, would be appropriate. The right to suspend employees should be written into the disciplinary procedures of the organisation.

Q12.8 How long can a "warning" stay in place?

A.   This will depend on the seriousness of the problem and what has been written into an organisation's disciplinary procedures. The employee's previous employment record and length of service may also be an influence. It is a matter of "reasonableness" on behalf of the employer. However, when taking disciplinary action, it is important to confirm to employees in writing what is expected of them, and this may well include a statement relating to the monitoring of behaviour over a set period of time (eg "timekeeping over the next three months"). If an employee had been well-behaved for a long period of time, and then "re-offended" you would have to start the formal disciplinary procedure again, with the employee having a "clean slate" in relation to written warnings. This again emphasises the need to have a thorough administrative system to support disciplinary matters.

Q12.9 What are my legal obligations regarding the disciplining and dismissal of employees?

A.   ACAS have produced a Code of Practice relating to disciplinary procedures. Whilst this is only advisory, it is good practice to follow these guidelines, and incorporate them into your own organisation's disciplinary procedures. In an Employment Tribunal, an employer would be expected to be familiar with the Code. Essentially you should give an employee a verbal warning (dependent on the nature of the problem), followed by a written warning and then a final written warning. It is important that the employee receives written confirmation of a disciplinary hearing, and that written warnings are issued as appropriate. The employee should sign a recognition of receipt of the warning, which would be made out in duplicate for the employer and employee. A common mistake often made is that an employee attends a meeting in which the employer has already prepared a warning letter without hearing the employees "side" of the story. This implies prejudgment of the situation and unwillingness to hear the employee's point of view. This could present problems in any subsequent claim to a tribunal.

If you dismiss an employee, then the need not to prejudge the situation is even more vital. The employee is entitled to receive a written reason for the dismissal. It is important to remember that this document could subsequently be used in any tribunal hearings.

Q12.10 If I have a disciplinary procedure, do I have to follow it even for very serious cases of misconduct?

A.   Yes. Your disciplinary rules and procedures should cover misconduct and gross misconduct. The major difference is that, whilst a "capability" problem may require you to give employees some time to improve, in the case of misconduct the employee is able to resolve the problem immediately by changing his or her behaviour.

In a case of gross misconduct, there is not the need for warnings, as gross misconduct is seen to be so serious that warnings would be inappropriate.

However, in this case it is important that the employer is seen to be reasonable, and this is usually demonstrated in two ways:

- by allowing the person to state their case
- if necessary, suspending the employee on full pay while a full investigation is carried out.

It can be very detrimental to a case to allow an employee to continue to work during this investigation, as this seems to imply that the "offence" committed really wasn't all that serious.

13. DISMISSAL

Q13.1 **If staff are dismissed incorrectly, I understand that this could be seen to be "wrongful" dismissal or "unfair" dismissal. What is the difference?**

A.   Essentially *wrongful dismissal* would be related to a contractual matter, and hence come under "common law". *Unfair dismissal*, however, would be in breach of legislation (**Employment Rights Act 1996**). In the past common law breaches would have been heard in the civil courts, the others being heard at a tribunal. However, tribunals can now hear civil matters relating to employment. In reality, the most common breach of employment contract relates to inappropriate periods of notice, and perhaps errors in payment of holiday entitlement to dismissed employees.

Q13.2 **What are the reasons for "fair dismissal" of an employee?**

A.   The right not to be unfairly dismissed is now consolidated into the provisions of the **Employment Rights Act 1996**.

The legislation confers the right not to be dismissed unfairly, provided that the employee has been employed for the required period of time, and is not older than the relevant age specified. The "fair" reasons for dismissal under s.57(1) are as follows.

1.   *Capability*: a reason related to the capability or qualifications of the employee performing the work of the kind which he or she was employed by the employer to do. "Capability" is assessed by reference to skill, aptitude, health, or any other physical or mental ability. "Qualifications" means any degree, diploma, or other academic, technical or professional qualification relevant to the position which the employee held.

2.   *Misconduct*: a reason related to the conduct of the employee.

3.   *Redundancy*: that the employee was redundant. The detail of redundancy will be dealt with in another section of the guide.

4. *Contravention of Enactment*: that the employee could not continue to work in that position that he or she held without contravention (either on his or her part or the employer) of a duty or restriction imposed by or under an enactment.

5. *Some other substantial reason.*

Section 61 of the Act stipulates an example of this concept which relates to employees who are replacements for employees who are absent through pregnancy or maternity leave. They can be fairly dismissed on the employee's return. Cases which have had this reason accepted include the expiry of a fixed-term contract and the frustration of a contract through the imprisonment of an employee. However, each case would have to be considered on its own merits (some other substantial reason).

The onus is on the employer to prove the reasons for dismissal, and if unable to do so, then the dismissal may be deemed to be unfair. It is important that the employer is seen to act reasonably at all times, and, for example, makes all house and disciplinary rules known to all employees. Also, it should provide training for employees who are performing poorly, and also give them an opportunity to improve their performance. In addition it is important the employer acts equitably with all employees, and is consistent in dealing with breaches of discipline.

Q13.3 **Has the Disability Discrimination Act affected any of the guidance on "incapability" dismissals?**

A. There have been cases where a person who had become physically incapable of carrying out their work, who might become able to be classified as "disabled". Employers could then be seen to be guilty of discrimination against particular employees in contravention of the **Disability Discrimination Act 1995**.

In the case of *Quinlan v B&Q* (1998 IDS 614:EAT), a man who had had a major operation became incapable of carrying large bags, which was a part of his normal duties. The tribunal ruled that he was not disabled within the terms of the Act, as he could lift many other things. Quinlan's discrimination claim failed, and the decision was upheld by the Employment Appeal Tribunal.

Q13.4   Which employees are protected against unfair dismissal?

A.   Currently this is all employees, regardless of hours worked, who have worked for an employer continuously for 104 weeks. The new Government, under its *Fairness at Work* white paper, has proposed that the qualifying period for protection against unfair dismissal be reduced to 52 weeks. It has been argued that the two year qualifying period is discriminatory as many women take employment for periods shorter than this, and hence have received no protection from unfair dismissal.

There has also been a growing trend in employment to recruit employees on short-term contracts of less than two years, employees who would of course receive no protection from unfair dismissal in addition to not being able to earn any potential rights to State redundancy pay.

This has meant that in some cases there have also been two classes of employee — those who have general employment protection, and those who do not. This could also lead to a situation in which different employees are treated differently from others, as the longer-serving employees have far more rights.

Q13.5   When the one year rule takes effect, will it be retrospective?

A.   Anyone with 52 weeks' service will be protected from unfair dismissal. Staff who had more than one year's service who have now left will not be able to make a claim. However, there are a number of cases currently pending with employees who have service between one and two years. A ruling in *Davidson v City Electrical* (1998 IRLR 108:EAT) the tribunal held that any employee who has this amount of service should have their cases adjourned, pending a European Court of Justice decision on this issue.

Q13.6 What is meant by "constructive dismissal"?

A.   In a case of constructive dismissal, there is no formal dismissal of the employee by the employer, but the Act treats certain acts of the employer as a dismissal.

Each individual case would, of course, have to be looked at on its merits, but the legislation attempts to protect employees against being forced to resign by the unreasonable action of their employer. There would normally have to be a fundamental breach of the contract by the employer for it to be seen as constructive dismissal. Often contracts are not written down and therefore this can be difficult to prove. It is for the employee to prove that he or she has been dismissed and, in the case of constructive dismissal, he or she must prove the term on which he or she relies in order to show that there has been a breach of contract by the employer.

A recent case *Waltons and Morse v Dorrington* (EAT) provided an interesting development on constructive dismissal. Mrs Dorrington had complaints about poor air quality at work brought about by others smoking in the building. She continued to complain about this for three years before she left her employment. The EAT ruled that the employer's action in requiring her to sit in a smoke-filled room affected her welfare to work. They stated that the employer had failed to address Mrs Dorrington's grievance, which was seen as a breach of contract, and that she had the right to resign and claim constructive dismissal.

Q13.7 In what types of case will dismissal be automatically "unfair"?

A.   In general, any cases that involve any form of discrimination: racial, or on the grounds of gender. Also to dismiss on the grounds of belonging to, or participating in the activities of a trade union, would also be unfair. Dismissal on grounds related to an employee's pregnancy would also be automatically unfair.

Q13.8   What is the basis of calculation of compensation in a case of unfair dismissal?

A.   Generally, there are three possible remedies in the case of unfair dismissal: reinstatement of the employee, re-engagement, or an award of compensation.

Compensation can consist of a "basic award", a compensatory award and, in cases where the tribunal requires reinstatement or re-engagement and the employer refuses, an "additional" award. There may also be a "special" award for dismissals relating to trade union and health and safety reasons.

In the *Fairness at Work* white paper, there are proposals that the limits on compensation for unfair dismissal be removed. However, currently this is not the case and the details are as follows.

1.   *Basic award:* the basic award is calculated as for redundancy pay, that is to say:

  – 1 week's pay for each year of employment between the ages of 22–41

  – 1.5 week's pay for the each year of employment over the age of 41

  – 0.5 week's pay for each year of employment under the age of 21.

The government sets the maximum weekly pay that is calculable, and there is a maximum calculable service of 20 years. If the dismissal took place after an employee's 64th birthday, the compensation would be reduced by 12 equal parts for each month over the age of 64, thus having no award as soon as the age of 65 is reached.

To establish continuous service, the employer should establish the effective date of termination of the employee, and then count backwards the number of completed years of service, subject to a maximum of 20.

The maximum calculable weekly wage is currently £220, hence the maximum award would be £6,600 (20 × 1.5 × £220).

2. *Compensatory award*: this is the sum that the tribunal feels is just and equitable, having regard to the losses sustained by the employee in consequence of the dismissal, in so far as that loss is attributable to the action taken by the employer. This loss would include any expenses reasonably incurred by the employee in consequence of the dismissal, and loss of any benefit which might reasonably be expected, had the dismissal not taken place. Currently the amount of a compensatory award may not exceed £11,000.

    The tribunal will consider normal benefits, such as the value of a company car when making its calculations.

    The employee has the normal common law obligation, that is to mitigate the losses involved.

3. *Additional award*: this could be awarded by the tribunal when an order of reinstatement or re-engagement is not complied with. If the reason for dismissal was for unlawful sexual or racial discrimination, the award will be for between 26 and 52 weeks' salary. In other cases it will be for between 13 and 26 weeks' salary.

4. *Special awards*: in the case of union-related dismissals, or certain health and safety dismissals, a special award may be made by the tribunal unless the complainant does not seek reinstatement or re-engagement. Such awards will not be made if the employee has unreasonably refused an offer of suitable alternative employment.

    The special award maximum currently stands at 104 weeks' salary with a maximum cash value set each year. If the tribunal makes an order of reinstatement or re-engagement, and this is not complied with, the compensation is increased to a maximum of 156 weeks pay, (no ceiling).

Q13.9   Do tribunals have "remedies" other than compensation?

A.   Yes. They can recommend or order reinstatement or re-engagement of the employee. The employer, however, does not have to accept this, but may have to pay an additional award to the employee by so doing. In practice, employers rarely re-engage staff or reinstate staff (the latter retaining full employment rights) and opt to pay the additional award.

Q13.10 Can I dismiss any employee for persistent genuine illness?

A.   Yes, as this could be justified on the grounds of "incapability". However, such cases need to be handled very carefully. The EAT has suggested that the following factors be taken into account when considering such cases:

- length of service
- length of future potential employment
- nature of the job
- length and effect of illness
- need for the work to be done
- risk of acquiring obligations to a replacement employee
- whether wages are still being paid
- acts and statements of the employee
- whether a reasonable employer could be expected to wait any longer
- contractual provision for sick pay
- prospects of recovery.

(*Williams v Watsons Luxury Coaches Ltd* 1990 IRLR 164).

Q13.11 What is the difference between dismissal and summary dismissal?

A.   A summary dismissal is a dismissal without the usual periods of notice, that is "instant dismissal". This would normally apply for very serious misconduct, and should be specified in the organisation's rules. Theft or violent behaviour often falls into this category. Nevertheless it is important that such behaviour is fully investigated and that the "offender" is given an opportunity to fully state his or her case before any action is taken. Employers should also consider a right to suspend employees pending investigation is such serious cases.

Q13.12 If I dismiss an employee for theft at work, and he or she is subsequently found "not guilty" in a criminal court, do I have to take the employee back?

A.   No. Any tribunal would simply consider the reasonableness of your actions in the light of information that you had to hand at the time of the dismissal. You would be expected, of course, to have carried out a full investigation, and listened to the employee's views, before taking your action to dismiss.

Q13.13 Can I dismiss staff without notice?

A.   Yes, if your statement of terms and conditions says you can; for example, in the case of gross misconduct by the employee. A full investigation would have been carried out before such action occurred, and it is vital that the employee is given the opportunity to state his or her case before any decisions about the employee's future employment are taken.

14. TERMINATING CONTRACTS

Q14.1 How can I terminate a contract of employment?

A. There are five main reasons for fair dismissal set out in Q13.2. One reason is the category of "some other substantial reason" may be the termination of a fixed-term contract.

Q14.2 Can I restrict who my employees work for after they leave my employment?

A. Many employers are concerned that a key employee, such as a sales manager, a chef or head waiter will compete with them should they leave. Employers therefore write restrictive covenants into employment contracts, the effect of which is to restrict the type of employment and/or geographical area in which an ex-employee can work for a specified period of time. For such a restrictive covenant to be upheld it will have to be shown that some specific interest is being protected, such as trade secrets or customers' names. Such actions carried out merely to prevent competition from the former employee will not be upheld (*Office Angels Ltd v Rainer-Thomas & O'Connor* (1991) IRLR 124).

Q14.3 Can an employee resign without giving notice?

A. In normal circumstances, an employment contract can be terminated by the employee by resigning within the terms of the contract. Should an employee resign without giving proper notice and in circumstances which are not in response to a repudiatory breach by the employer, the employee is in breach of contract and, strictly speaking, could be sued for damages.

However, where an employer has taken steps which are perceived by the employee to be a breach of contract (express or implied) the employee may resign without giving notice, possibly claiming constructive dimissal. Furthermore, dependent upon the circumstances, there may be grounds for bringing an action for unfair dismissal or even wrongful dismissal.

Q14.4   Can I dismiss staff without notice?

A.   Yes, if your statement of terms and conditions or your disciplinary rules say you can, for example in the case of gross misconduct. However, a full investigation would have to be carried out before such action occurred (see Q13.11).

Q14.5   Can an employer withdraw notice once it has been given?

A.   Notice of dismissal, once given, cannot be unilaterally withdrawn by the employer unless the employee agrees.

Q14.6   Can an employee withdraw his or her notice once it has been given?

A.   In the same way that notice of dismissal cannot be unilaterally withdrawn by the employer, a resignation also cannot be withdrawn, once given, unless the employer agrees. The exception to this rule is where an employee gives notice in the heat of the moment. Employers are advised not to accept a resignation given in the heat of the moment without some cooling-off period, as this could possibly be construed as constructive dismissal.

Q14.7   In the event of an offence being committed by a new employee, do I need to use the disciplinary procedures or can I simply terminate their employment?

A.   Effectively the first four weeks of employment are regarded as a trial period and no notice period is required during this period (ERA 1996), thereafter one week's notice is required per year's length of service. "Express terms" in the main statement of terms and conditions of employment may override this and contain an extended probationary period and make provision for more generous periods of notice. If a disciplinary offence is committed and of a sufficiently serious nature in the early stages of employment, the preceding factors should be borne in mind and a decision made as to whether it is of more value to follow a course of disciplinary action or not.

It must be remembered that it is also stated within the ERA 1996 that it is automatically unfair to dismiss on the grounds of:

- pregnancy, and
- trade union membership
- from the commencement of employment.

See also answer to Q13.7.

Q14.8   **What does a "frustrated" contract mean?**

A.   A frustrated contract indicates that the contract has come to an end where through no fault of either party the contract becomes impossible to perform, or if performed it would result in something radically different from what was originally intended. In the employment field this would mean a termination without a dismissal or resignation. This may occur in, for example, the case of an employee's permanent incapacity to work. This could also apply in the event of an employee being imprisoned (*FC Shepherd & Co Ltd v Jerrom* (1986) IRLR 358).

15. EMPLOYMENT (INDUSTRIAL) TRIBUNALS

Q15.1 **Does the change in title mean than Employment Tribunals now have a new role?**

A.   Not really, there was a change in jurisdiction brought about by the **Industrial Tribunals Extensions of Jurisdiction (England and Wales) Order 1994** (SI 1994 No.1623) and the **Industrial Tribunals Extensions of Jurisdiction (Scotland) Order 1994** (SI 1994 No.1624) which enabled employees to bring contractual claims to a tribunal where the subject of the claim arises from the termination of employment. In the past, tribunals were not able to deal with common law claims even if they arose in an employment context. For example, the same facts may have given rise to a claim for unfair dismissal in a tribunal, and a claim for wrongful dismissal in the county court. It could have been that an employee had to bring two claims in different places, and this anomaly has now been partly removed. There are some restrictions on common law claims, which involves a £25,000 ceiling on claims, and the tribunal is not able to deal with matters relating to restrictive covenants on future employment, or on matters relating to the provision of accommodation. These must still go to the county court. Under certain circumstances, the **Industrial (Employment) Tribunals Act 1996** does give "the appropriate Minister" the power to confer further jurisdiction on Industrial (Employment) Tribunals. At the time of writing there is some discussion about the role of tribunals being undertaken by arbitrators, in an attempt to simplify the system. However, current proposals do not include the right to appeal, that is to say an arbitrator's decision would be final. This is the cause of some debate and may change before a final decision is taken.

Q15.2 **As a number of employment matters now appear to be influenced by European Union law, has this affected the scope of**

cases covered by an employment tribunal? Does it include European Law?

A.   Tribunals have historically dealt with employment matters such as unfair dismissal, discrimination in employment, equal pay (value), Wages Act claims and issues relating to trade unions. They have no powers except those given by Acts of Parliament. However, the **European Communities Act 1972** gives them the obligation to apply European law when dealing with matters over which they have jurisdiction. What this means in practice is that tribunals must apply any relevant EU law which applies to a particular claim, such as one for unfair dismissal. Thus the original claim must be brought under UK legislation, but the relevance of EU law will be considered. For example, in the area of transfer of undertaking legislation, EU law and judgments has a major influence on tribunal judgments.

Q15.3   I understand that "out of court settlements" on employment matters may not be binding — is that correct?

A.   The general rule is that such agreements are not binding and can not prevent an employee from making a claim to a tribunal. However, the exception would be by the use of a compromise agreement, introduced in 1993. Such agreements have to meet a number of conditions as follows:

- they should be in writing
- they must relate to a particular complaint
- the employee must have received advice from a lawyer about the effect of the proposed agreement on his or her rights to pursue a claim in a tribunal
- the lawyer concerned must be covered by professional indemnity insurance
- the lawyer concerned should be identified in the agreement
- the lawyer should be "independent", ie not acting for the employer

- the lawyer concerned must be qualified as a barrister or a solicitor with a practising certificate
- the agreement must state that all these conditions are satisfied.

In addition, in the circumstances where a conciliation officer has been involved in trying to promote a settlement between an employer and an employee, that officer may draw up an agreement. This would make the agreement enforceable, and would prevent the applicant from pursuing the claim in a tribunal. It can only take place after there has been an originating application to an Employment Tribunal. Following the agreement, the conciliation officer will endorse the settlement on a form, known as the COT.3.

These rules do not apply to common law claims, and thus an out-of-court settlement of a *contract claim* is fully binding and can prevent proceedings either in a court or tribunal.

Q15.4 **Does a former employee have to tell me that they intend to pursue a claim in a tribunal, and how long after they have left me can they do this?**

A.   An employee has to file a claim, such as one for unfair dismissal within three months of the date of dismissal. Such forms are usually available from JobCentres, and thus the first you may be aware of a claim is when you receive a document asking you to respond to that claim. Employees have the right to ask for a written reason for dismissal, and it is important that this is completed with some care, in case of subsequent claims. Thus the real reason for dismissal should be stated, one that can be supported with appropriate evidence.

Q15.5 **I have been called to attend an Employment Tribunal as a result of a claim from a former employee. What processes are involved in this?**

A.   These are outlined below and it should be noted that in an attempt to reduce the number of insubstantial cases being heard, new regulations have been brought in. The **Industrial Tribunals (Constitution and Rules Procedure) Regulations 1993** were introduced as a result of TURERA 1993.

1. An Employment Tribunal case is commenced by the employee ("applicant") presenting an application to the Central Office of Employment Tribunals. This is often done on an originating application form (IT1). This will tell you the basis of the claim.

2. The employer (respondent) will receive a copy of this, and has fourteen days in which to respond. It is possible to request an extension of time in which to respond to this, and the tribunal will decide if this is possible.

    It may be that you require further information to carry out your investigation, and you can ask for "further and better" particulars from the other party.

3. There will be a pre-hearing review, and if the tribunal feels that the claimant, or the employer, has little chance of success it can ask for a deposit of up to £150 to be paid. This is intended to discourage unnecessary claims and tribunal hearings. The tribunal may decide to undertake this review, or it could be done at the request of one of the parties. Witnesses will not be called at such a review.

4. The tribunal hearing is a public hearing and the tribunal usually consists of three people, although the chairperson may now sit alone. In case of unfair dismissal where the dismissal is admitted, and the employee qualifies to make a claim, the employer will then take on the burden of proof to show that the dismissal was fair. The party will briefly outline the case and will introduce witnesses and appropriate documentary evidence, such as written warnings, and copies of house rules, statements of terms and conditions, etc. The member(s) of the panel have the right to examine and cross-examine each witness. When all witnesses have been called, there is a right to make a closing speech.

The tribunal will then make a decision. The reasons are usually given in summary form, but extended reasons can be requested within 21 days of receipt of the summary reasons.

5.   Any party has the right to appeal against a decision on a point of law to the Employment Appeals Tribunal (EAT) within 42 days of receipt of the extended reasons for the tribunal decision.

Q15.6   What "remedies" can a tribunal take if an employee's claim is proven?

A.   It will usually award compensation, but can also make an order to reinstate or re-engage the employee. If such an order is refused, then the tribunal may make an additional award. Financial compensation is awarded in several ways. There is a basic award, which is calculated in the same way as for statutory redundancy pay (a combination of the claimant's age and length of service), and has a current maximum of £6600. A compensatory award of up to £12,000 can be made regarding expenses incurred or loss of earnings, and in some circumstances, such as the refusal to reinstate an employee when it has been ordered, could result in an additional award. Cases involving discrimination usually carry larger penalties.

Q15.7   If an employee pursues a case in a tribunal, what documentation might I need, and would any official documentation be required?

A.   As stated above, evidence to support your case, such as written warnings, records of disciplinary hearings and appeals, copies of your disciplinary procedures, terms and conditions of employment, house rules, evidence of training, evidence of absences, etc, dependent on the nature of the claim.

Q15.8   Do I need a lawyer to act on my behalf in a tribunal?

A.   Not usually. Tribunal procedures have been made simple to allow employees and employers to present their own cases. However, if there are complicated legal concepts involved, then it is advisable to take legal advice, and possibly representation.

Q15.9   If I do not agree with the judgment of a tribunal, is it possible to appeal against the decision?

A.   Yes, but only on a point of law. This would be made to the Employment Appeal Tribunal (EAT).

Q15.10 Are costs awarded in a tribunal in the same way as courts?

A.   Not usually. Only if the tribunal feels that in either bringing the case or in conducting the hearing, one party has acted frivolously, vexatiously or otherwise unreasonably will costs be charged.

INDEX

A

absenteeism 62

Access to Medical Reports Act 1988 61

accidents 78, 80

accommodation
employers' rights 45–46
and National Minimum Wage 43
tax 53

Acquired Rights Directive 104, 105, 107

Advisory, Conciliation and Arbitration Service (ACAS)
Code of Disciplinary Practice and Procedure 32, 117, 119, 120–121
Code of Practice on Disclosure of Information 99
Code of Practice on Redundancy 110

age discrimination 5–6

AIDS 81–82

all-employee share option schemes 56

alternative employment 113, 114
trial periods 115–116

amoebic dysentery 80

annual leave 44–45, 94

antenatal care 63–64

appearance 3–4

application forms 1–2

Asylum and Immigration Act 1996 14–15

Attachment of Earnings orders 48

average weekly wage 114–115

Avon County Council v Howlett 46

Ayse Suzen v Zehnacker Gebaudereinigung GmbH Krankenhausservice and Lefarth GmbH 106, 107

B

bacillary dysentery 80

backhanders 23

beards 3

Bellhaven Brewery Co. Ltd v McClean 74

benefits
National Minimum Wage 43
share option schemes 56
tax 53
transfer of undertakings 105

Bland v Stockport Borough Council 84

board and lodging *see* accommodation

J

K

L

M